TAKE BETTER PHOTOGRAPHS

Michael Busselle

PEERAGE BOOKS

CONTENTS

First published in Great Britain in 1979 by
Octopus Books Ltd

This edition published in 1984 by
Peerage Books
59 Grosvenor Street
London W1

© 1979 Octopus Books Ltd

ISBN 0 907408 91 5

Printed in Hong Kong

INTRODUCTION

Photography has become, in a rather quiet and unassuming way, a major influence on our lives during this century. With cinemas and television, books and magazines, it dominates a large proportion of our entertainment and its role in education and information services is irreplaceable. In addition to its social importance, photography has also become one of our most popular and accessible hobbies providing both a very satisfying means of recording and preserving our most memorable experiences and also offering a rewarding means of self-expression.

Because of this, it is particularly unfortunate that a feeling has grown amongst casual camera users that whilst it is relatively easy to take snap shots, it is much more difficult and expensive to produce good photography, which is thought to require complex and costly equipment as well as a vast store of technical knowledge.

This is simply not true, and the difference between a snap shot and a good photograph is usually just a little extra thought and care. This is all that is needed to progress from being a casual snapshotter who is frequently disappointed with his results to a photographer who can be proud of his efforts. It is not even necessary to learn new skills – one only needs to apply the same degree of observation and awareness to taking a picture that most people use every day in other areas of their lives and it is surprising how quickly and dramatically the pictures will improve.

The intention in the planning of this book has been to show how often by a simple change of viewpoint – the way a picture is framed or by the use of a simple technique – an otherwise average snap can be changed into a good photograph.

MICHAEL BUSSELLE

THE CAMERA

Many people still cling to the mythical notion that the pinhole camera fathered the modern camera. In fact, photographic cameras started out in much the same form, albeit primitive, as many simple cameras today. The familiar components of lens, aperture, focussing and shutter were all there, although you might not recognize them immediately. Most of the development of the camera as we know it took place when it was still the *camera obscura*, (literally the 'dark room') used by sightseers and artists since the 11th century. It was the camera obscura, projecting its shadowy image of the external world, which first used the pinhole, and it was artists who were responsible for introducing optical lenses to produce a focussed, upright image.

The pioneers of photography did not think backwards and invent a camera to use the process they devised. They invented their process in order to capture the image provided by a camera obscura without having to draw it. The camera existed before photography and not vice versa. Naturally, early photographers like Louis Daguerre (1787–1851) and W.H. Fox Talbot (1800–1877) used the brightest and best small 'cameras' they could make or have made. Even so, the processes were so insensitive to light that the early shutter was simply a cover for the lens, in effect a lens cap. With exposures of 30 minutes this was perfectly adequate, and continued to be so for many years. The method is still used in some types of photography. The early camera used a single convex or meniscus lens with its outer, optically inaccurate area masked off so that only a central 'hole' passed the image-forming light. Its 'film' took the form of rigid metal, glass plates, or paper which could be fixed inside the back of the camera, and only gave one single exposure at a time, so no special holders or loading techniques were needed. The camera was just a box with film at one end and a lens at the other. In fact, it still is.

Camera design progressed in a series of jumps. With the first processes it was obvious that the biggest initial improvement would be to pare down the exposure time. So while the cameras stayed basically the same, work was done on film sensitivity. Very soon this work was so successful that cameras could be used anywhere. Better focussing and viewing arrangements were needed. The lens cap shutter was unsuitable for short exposures of a second or two, so simple mechanical open-close shutters were made. Then optical design took big steps forward and lenses became 'fast' enough to transmit bright pictures, and instantaneous pictures (instant exposure time) became practical. So shutters of various sprung or gravity types were made to control times such as 1/10 or 1/4 second. Cameras developed to become even more portable and suitable for hand-held use. Methods for loading plates in daylight and viewing on a focussing screen were standardized. Further advances in film manufacture gave us in rapid succession, even better hand-held results and the first roll-film. Similar advances in printing papers made enlargement from small negatives more possible popularly. Once the camera moved permanently to the hand from the tripod, today's fast shutter speeds began to appear on complex shutters, and accurate viewing and focussing systems became a standard part of many cameras.

From this stage, just after World War I, optical design, film manufacturing technology and camera design jostled each other forward. Compact 35 mm cameras made unobtrusive photography popular; unobtrusive photography called for success in all kinds of poor light without extra illumination; that demanded fast lenses and high speed film with reasonable quality; fast lenses demanded highly accurate focussing; small film sizes demanded that every square millimetre of film be used, with no waste; this in turn called for accurate viewfinding and interchangeable lenses to frame up precisely.

Each new advance presented further opportunities for enthusiasts. Within a very short space of time from the invention of photography cameras had been successfully attached to telescopes and microscopes, used underwater, made exposures by electrical 'flash' discharges, taken 3D pictures, made colour transparencies, and done all kinds of unexpected things. Today these things are all possible relatively easily with most popular cameras but the primary uses of the camera are far more mundane. You may have a choice of a hundred different possible settings on your camera, but it's very likely that the settings you use most often could be identical to those used by a photographer in the 1870s—perhaps using the latest equipment and materials for his day. The difference between you and him lies in the scores of other available settings which enable you to tackle photographs he could not have considered possible, and the fact that he would have been an expert. Today's photographer need not be.

How it works

You cannot form a photographic image of an object without manipulating the light it reflects. Light may travel in straight lines, but it also radiates in all directions equally, diverging as it travels. You won't catch it without help.

To form an image, that radiating divergent light must be channeled to duplicate the relative positions of its sources. One way to do this is to take just one narrow beam of light from each part of the subject and ignore all the other diverging beams. You can do this with a pinhole which allows only a narrow ray of light through from each point. The resulting image, made up from a very limited amount of the total original light, is extremely dim. A far better way is to use a convex optical lens to take a whole bundle of diverging rays from each point on the subject and bend them back again to converge once more at a point. The result is an image in which each 'point' is the result of many coinciding rays, not just one. It is far brighter than a pinhole image, but the geometry is identical.

The process of bending those diverging light rays back to a point is called 'focussing' and the point is called 'their focus'.

Now we have a way of producing a sharp, focussable image with a lens. If we build a lightproof box behind that lens, no stray light can interfere with the picture produced. Place a light sensitive sheet of film in that box, without allowing any other light to fall on it at any time, and you have the camera. But film has a *fixed* sensitivity to light depending on its type. If we are going to show grey as grey and black as black, there must be some difference in their effect on the film. So the lens must be fitted with a shutter to allow light in only for the correct time. The shutter may be in front of the film, inside the lens, or even in front of the lens—as long as it cuts off light properly,

As well as the time of exposure, the brightness of the overall scene can be varied. This is done by changing the physical diameter of the lens so that a narrow cone, a smaller bundle, of light rays is focussed. As you can't change the size of the actual lens, you cut down the diameter by placing next to it a metal 'stop' with an aperture hole cut in the centre.

This is the complete camera in fundamental form. A lightproof box holding the film at one end, with a lens to focus light rays from the world outside at the other; a focussing control to move the lens and ensure that the focus of those rays coincides exactly with the film; a shutter to keep out the light except when needed for the exposure; an aperture to control or adjust the brightness of the image on the film by cutting down on the amount of light; and a viewfinder to show the user what the camera is seeing.

The majestic, old, wooden camera has resulted in the development of the sophisticated single lens reflex camera and the compact completely automatic cartridge camera.

The large format camera

Sometimes called the 'view camera', or 'technical camera', the modern large format camera is normally a professionals-only studio instrument designed to take sheets of 5 × 4 inch film, which are inserted in darkslide holders individually. There is no viewfinder, and the picture is focussed up on a ground glass screen at the rear of the camera using the familiar 'watch the birdie' dark cloth to cut out bright surrounding light. A tripod is essential and the working methods with a 5 × 4 most closely resemble those of an early photographer.

The large format camera allows interchanging of lenses as freely as a 35 mm reflex, if not more so. You can also change the whole shape of the camera, so that back and front are no longer parallel or directly in line. These 'movements' allow precise corrections of sharpness, perspective and the shape of the subject as seen on the film. The requirements of large format work are very different from rollfilm and 35 mm work, calling for extremely small apertures. This means that a studio environment is essential; large format cameras are rarely suitable for use without such facilities.

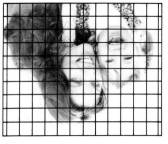

What you see through a large format plate or half plate camera is the image of your subject upside down. There is no viewfinder, the image is focussed on a ground glass screen at the back of the camera. Grid lines on the screen help the photographer to compose the upside down picture.

Simple basic camera

The simplest form of camera has a fixed lens, preset to a suitable focus, a fixed shutter speed and aperture and nothing else apart from the means to load and advance the film. This was the form of the familiar old box camera and still is the form of the popular 110 pocket camera at its simplest.

The basic camera usually has a single glass or plastic lens of about f.13 and a spring-loaded simple shutter which gives an exposure of about 1/50 second, which is suitable for sunny summer days, slightly hazy sun, and bright sun in winter, and

The simple 110 format camera has a direct viewfinder. You look through the viewer to frame up the image and the camera does the rest.

may also work in bright overcast light in summer, with normal film. The only important aspects of the camera are how well the lens is set into its mount to focus on about one and a half metres, and how closely the viewfinder window approximates the final picture seen on the film.

Viewfinder camera

Available in almost all film sizes, the viewfinder camera may be loaded with as many adjustments and refinements as you are willing to pay for. All viewfinder cameras use a separate optical system to view the scene which the lens is also covering. Normally, the photographer has to set the distance of the main part of the subject on the lens focussing scale, either by measurement or by guesswork. Viewfinder cameras are used at eye level and when held to the eye the controls and settings are usually not visible.

Because the viewfinder itself is sharp and bright it is easy to forget that this is not the optical system responsible for the photograph, and to omit to set the correct focus and exposure on the lens. It's also fatally easy to let a finger obscure the lens without seeing this in the finder or, classic howler, to leave a lens cap on.

What you see through a viewfinder camera is not always what you get. The framing lines in the viewer indicate the extent of the image, but focussing is separate.

Rangefinder camera

Like the standard viewfinder, the rangefinder uses a direct viewing system, but also has a system for measuring distance built in to its viewing optics. This may take the form of a central spot in which the detail of the scene in front appears to be split into two ghost images which only coincide when the lens is correctly adjusted to focus on the appropriate distance. This type of viewfinder generally has to be made to a high degree of accuracy in other ways as well, with more precise frame markings and some means of moving the framed area as the lens is focussed for close-ups, to compensate for parallax error (the difference in position between the viewfinder and the lens which results in different viewpoints and cut-off subject matter).

In the Leica system, the most important rangefinder system, lenses are also interchangeable and their differing fields of view are shown in the finder. Rangefinder models are available in most sizes, but most are 35 mm.

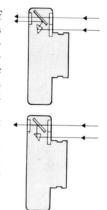

Rangefinders are focussing aids for direct viewfinder cameras. What you see through the viewer is two images: one direct and the second 'ghost' image via a system of mirrors one of which is linked to the focussing ring. When the focus is perfectly adjusted the two images become one.

Instant camera

All instant picture systems are limited by the fact that the picture has to be photographed on a fairly large sheet of film to produce a print big enough to be satisfactory, about 3×4 inch being standard. This makes the cameras larger than other popular types. Many are viewfinder cameras, some with rangefinders, and some are reflex cameras. The reflex models use unconventional systems or mirrors and lenses to 'fold' the shape of the camera to an acceptable size. The designs may be rigid or folding.

There are two further distinguishing points: cameras either accept 'dry' materials (colour only) or 'peel apart' prints (many types) but not both together, and photographs may be removed by hand or a motorized system.

viewfinder polaroid

Most instant cameras are direct viewfinders, featuring various focussing aids from simple graphic symbols on the camera body to complete rangefinder systems. Reflex polaroids use the same focussing as a standard SLR.

reflex polaroid

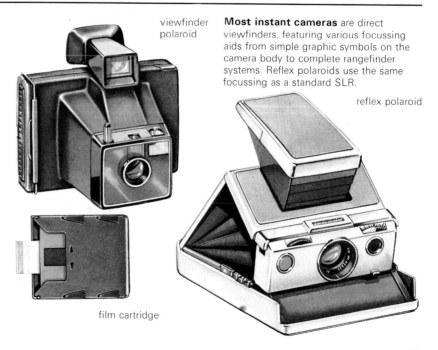

film cartridge

Twin lens reflex

Because the movement of the mirror is fairly slow, and depends on the size of glassware involved, early reflexes in large sizes, such as the $3\frac{1}{2} \times 4\frac{1}{2}$ inch format were very noisy and heavy. The mirror was lifted by a hand operated lever and often lowered manually as well. So the twin lens reflex (TLR) was invented, with a normal camera on its 'ground floor' and a camera with a fixed 45° mirror and ground glass screen top fixed above it. The two cameras had perfectly matched lenses making identical images. In this way the twin lens reflex imitated the reflex without moving mirrors.

Later, when cameras became smaller and 35 mm film established itself as the standard size, ordinary reflexes came back into fashion, with spring mechanisms operating their much lighter mirrors. The phrase 'single lens reflex' or SLR, distinguished these from the popular twin lens reflex.

What you see through a TLR is what you get, but reversed left to right. As you move the camera to frame your scene, the viewfinder image moves in the opposite direction, which can take some time to get used to. Grid lines are usually provided to help with composition. Most TLRs are held at waist level with the viewer mounted on top of the camera. However, if you are shooting sporting events or other fast moving subjects, you can fit a sportfinder to help you follow the movement. Alternatively, substitute a pentuprism for the TLR viewer and enjoy SLR viewing.

Unusual cameras

Apart from the usual kinds of cameras that dealers stock all the year round, you may encounter many specialized types. For example, most types of camera, except SLRs, are available with built-in flash. This has the advantage of convenience and the disadvantage of adding slightly to the bulk of the camera even when you don't need it may not equal the power of a separate flash. Many cameras also have autofocussing coupled to the lens, electronically measuring the subject distance of the nearest solid surface or of a surface lined up with a mark in the viewfinder.

Some cameras (notably Minox) take subminiature film in 16 mm or 8 mm sizes but these are often little smaller than 110 pocket cameras. They tend to offer higher precision and more sophisticated controls

and finish. Stereoscopic cameras such as Nimslo are available for making 3D prints. Underwater cameras range from the very simple 'Scubasnap' type, with a large housing containing a basic camera, through special housings for 110 and 35 mm cameras, to the Nikonos underwater 35 mm rangefinder model, which needs no additional housing and is fully sealed. Binocular cameras appear on the market regularly (the 110 Tasco Binocam for example) and consist of a pair of binoculars linked to a camera which may use the binocular lens or have one of its own.

Radio cameras and other 'compendium' novelties also appear from time to time, normally using the compact 110 film size to fit a camera in with another 'leisure' item. Disposable preloaded, idiot-proof cameras which are returned complete

for opening, film processing and reloading are sold during holiday seasons in many tourist areas for nothing more than the price of film and processing, and are very simple. Build-your-own cameras are available in sizes from 110 to 120 rollfilm as kits, but nothing is saved by buying one—the prices are much the same as for the equivalent assembled camera. Two-lens cameras are popular in the 110 size, with a normal lens and sliding close-up or telephoto lens built into the same body. Date printing cameras are available in 35 mm and use an internal optical system to 'print' the date or a reference number in the corner of each picture. Folding or collapsible cameras are available in all sizes from 110 to 6 × 7 cm and most of these form their own dustproof case when collapsed. The Agfa 110 and Minox 35 EL are examples.

The single lens reflex (SLR)

The SLR is now the standard 'serious' camera. 'Single lens reflex' is now a universal photographic term. Originally cameras of the same type were just called reflex cameras.

The reflex principle is very simple. Using a mirror, set at 45° to the incoming image-forming light, between the lens and the film, the picture is diverted and thrown on to a ground glass focussing screen on the camera top instead of onto the film itself. As all the distances and alignments are identical, the size and composition and focussing of the picture can be viewed on the glass in precisely the form that they will be captured on the film. To make the exposure, the mirror moves upwards where it blocks off the ground glass and seals out light. Now the camera is just a lightproof box with a lens at one end and film at the other, and the exposure is made as normal. The shutter is usually *behind* the mirror and near the film.

Today's single lens reflex (SLR), whether in 35 mm or rollfilm size, is intended to be used at eye level, with the viewing system acting very much like a viewfinder of the direct optical type. The best systems show the view in front virtually unchanged in clarity, brightness and size. Viewing through the lens, and having an optical system taking the image from the lens, makes two major things possible: first of all the adjustment of focus through the lens itself, and secondly the automatic framing up of the correct image size, as any additional optics or alternative lens fitted will project its own image through the finder.

An extra feature found on nearly all cameras is the measurement of light through the same system, either for use in manual adjustment of settings, or coupled directly for auto exposure. The 35 mm reflex tends to have the largest range of facilities and accessories, and the standard pattern is for a model to have automatic or manual exposure, speeds from roughly 1 to 1/1000 second lenses available from 28 mm to 200 mm, and provision for automatic film transport by an attached or built-in motor winder.

Today 'single lens' is possibly a deceptive phrase as the whole advantage of the SLR is that it can take more than one lens—many makes have ranges of 20 or more alternative, interchangeable lenses.

They use focal-plane shutters (positioned near the film) which totally block out light even when the camera lens is removed in full sunlight, so that the lenses are easily changed at any time.

The exact angle of view and focussing of each lens can be seen clearly on the focussing screen, aided by a system of prisms and magnifiers which give a bright, sharp picture. This is also the right way round, so that no extra viewfinders or rangefinders are needed. Close-up lenses, telescopes, microscopes and all kinds of optics can also be focussed accurately through the SLR.

Unlike fixed-lens cameras, SLRs are 'system cameras'. The modern SLR camera is normally backed up by a whole range of accessories. The SLR body is the heart of the system and will accept accessories in various ways: fitting the lens mount; fitting the eyepiece of the viewfinder, perhaps replacing the viewfinder itself; fitting the baseplate, to advance the film; replacing the camera back; fitting into the camera's accessory (flash) shoe.

Choose an SLR system if you want to use the camera for two or more purposes, or want to record all your subjects with just one camera.

The 35mm SLR is the most popular camera today. It is easy to use, as what you see through the viewer is exactly what you get on the final print. Focussing, aperture variation, depth of field and the effect of filters and lens attachments can all be assessed before you shoot, and the TTL metering system means that you have all your basic picture taking equipment in one compact package.

The standard SLR system

You see you have a great range of accessories to choose from. Some items are superfluous or too specialized for most users, but others are almost essential. Here is a suggested typical SLR system as owned and used by the average non-professional photographer with varied interest and a modest budget.

The Camera An auto-manual SLR with provision for a compact auto winder, a bayonet mount, and a compact standard lens of 40 mm focal length. The camera has shutter speeds from 1 to 1/1000 sec. which can be set manually, or pre-selection of the lens aperture and setting the shutter dial to auto gives a range from 8 to 1/1000 secs.

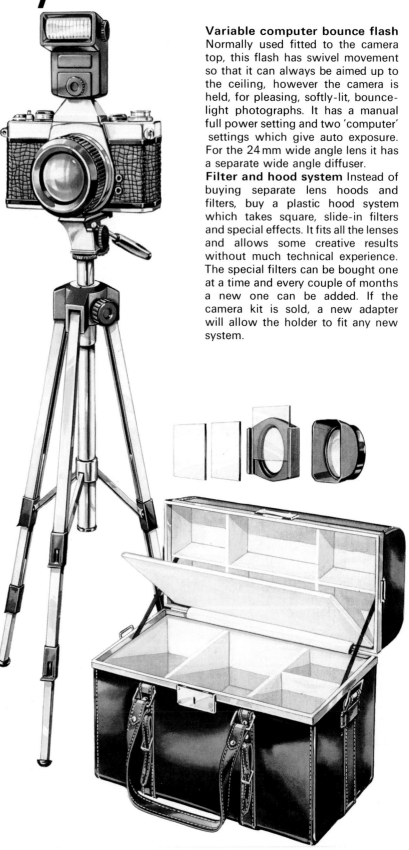

Wide angle lens A 24mm f.2.5 wide angle, not made by the camera manufacturer but still of high quality. Its mount can be changed should the camera ever be sold to buy a new one with a different fitting. The 24mm has been carefully chosen so that it takes the same size filters as the 40 mm standard.

Compact tele zoom lens A 70 to 150 mm f.3.8 zoom with a close-focussing facility, again from an independent maker, using the same interchangeable mount system and taking the same size filters. It has with it a matched 2X tele converter which costs very little but gives a 140 to 300 mm f.7 tele zoom when fitted. It can be used with the standard 40 mm and the resulting f.4 80 mm compact lens is fine for portraits.

Variable computer bounce flash Normally used fitted to the camera top, this flash has swivel movement so that it can always be aimed up to the ceiling, however the camera is held, for pleasing, softly-lit, bounce-light photographs. It has a manual full power setting and two 'computer' settings which give auto exposure. For the 24 mm wide angle lens it has a separate wide angle diffuser.

Filter and hood system Instead of buying separate lens hoods and filters, buy a plastic hood system which takes square, slide-in filters and special effects. It fits all the lenses and allows some creative results without much technical experience. The special filters can be bought one at a time and every couple of months a new one can be added. If the camera kit is sold, a new adapter will allow the holder to fit any new system.

The Exposure meter

Minipod and grip If you do not want to carry around a large tripod, buy a compact mini tripod contained in a pistol-grip with a small swivel ball-and-socket at the top. This is convenient outdoors and allows the camera to be placed on a table for self-portraits (often in groups) using the camera's delayed action release. The grip includes a simple G-clamp so that the camera may be fixed firmly to a door, table edge, or vertical surface when no flat area is available.

Holdall All the equipment, plus several rolls of film and a cleaning brush and cloth for the camera and lenses, fits into this shoulder bag which has padded divisions to prevent metal items damaging each other. The shoulder strap can be shortened to form a handle, and when the bag is over the shoulder it can be opened so the front drops down to form a flat platform with side, allowing a lens or camera body to rest safely on it while changing film or accessories, or cleaning items.

If you need to travel 80 kilometres you can drive for two hours at 40 kilometres per hour or 30 minutes at 160 kilometres per hour. The end result is the same. Exposing photographic film follows the same logic. To produce a certain shade of grey on the film, exactly the same exposure is always required: it does not vary. The shade of grey (or the depth and tone of colour) depends solely on the amount of light hitting the film, which determines how many silver compound crystals are eventually converted to silver. That light may arrive very slowly over a long period, or it may all 'come at once' in the form of brilliant illumination for a fraction of a second. Whichever way you do it, the total light-energy remains constant.

This constant gives us a fixed 'speed' for the film, and once you have one fixed figure the other variables can be easily worked out. The most obvious variable factor is the light itself, how bright the scene being photographed is. The sole function of the exposure meter is to measure the brightness of the scene. All photographic light meters have a calculator of some kind on them (or an electronic calculating circuit) which is first of all set to the ASA speed of the film being used. Then, when a light reading is taken, the calculator is moved or automatically set to that reading. The two scales then line up beside each other.

All modern exposure meters work on the principle that certain types of metal, or electronic devices, can generate or control an electric current depending on the level of light falling on them. Just as film is always equally affected by a given level of light, these electrical circuits are always affected to the same degree by a given brightness. So they can be equipped with a galvanometer (needle-type measuring system) or a readout (digital or light-balancing electronic measuring system) to indicate the brightness of the light. This reading is then transferred to the calculator scale of the meter and turned into f stops and shutter speeds to give correct exposure.

How to use the meter
The first snag you encounter when trying to measure light is a simple one. Imagine a black cat on a white road. An exposure meter pointed at the scene will be receiving a lot of bright light from the road. But how about the cat? If it runs on to a black side-road and we take a reading again, the amount of light will naturally appear to have fallen—there will be less reflected to the meter. And that happens even if the sun keeps shining without change. The light reflected from a scene depends on the *subject* as well as the illumination.

On film, we want to see black as black and white as white. If the

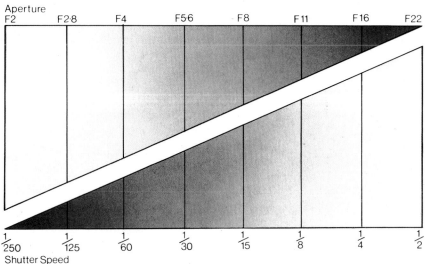

Exposure meters work by showing the correlation between shutter speed and f stops, and their changing relationship under different light conditions. As the light changes, necessary adjustments will be indicated.

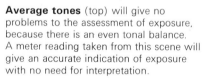

Average tones (top) will give no problems to the assessment of exposure, because there is an even tonal balance. A meter reading taken from this scene will give an accurate indication of exposure with no need for interpretation.

Underexposure will result from a reading taken in circumstances where the background predominates, such as this scene (centre left), unless allowance is made for the large area of white wall.

Underexposure is inevitable when large areas of sky are included in the meter reading zone (centre right). In normal circumstances, the meter should be tilted downwards when taking the reading to exclude the sky.

Overexposure will occur with pictures like this one (right) unless allowance is made for the large area of dark tones in the scene. A good way of avoiding this problem is to calculate an average reading.

meter reads a black subject it will tell us to increase exposure—to make that subject seem whiter on film. If it sees a white subject it tells us to cut down exposure, giving a grey result. In fact, all normal exposure meters 'integrate to grey'. They are designed to give a correct reading from an average grey tone, so they try to produce grey tones on the film even when the subject is mainly black or mainly white.

The actual grey for which meters are calibrated is 18% reflectance. That means that 18% of the light arriving ('incident' light) is reflected. Meters which work this way are called reflected light meters, and this includes all built-in meters in cameras. There is another kind of meter called an 'incident light' meter which is aimed at the source of light itself (or more precisely at the camera from the subject position), and this is free from the problems of integrating all subjects to turn out as grey. It is a little harder to use and can not always be used from the camera position.

However, once you grasp that a light meter is designed to read from a grey average tone it is easy to take a quick light-reading from a hand, a jacket, or from a small part of the subject which is of average tone. With experience, you will come to know that if a reading is taken from a very dark-toned subject it is necessary to give only one quarter of the indicated exposure, or that if a reading is taken from a white subject two and a half times the indicated exposure should be given.

How to use the meter

Where a hand held exposure meter simply scans a given angle such as 20°, a built-in meter in an SLR takes in a certain amount of the viewing screen. How it balances the area of the screen makes a lot of difference to readings. An averaging meter (integrated light reading) will take an even reading over the whole screen: all parts have equal importance. A spot meter will probably only read from a small circle indicated in the centre of the screen. A centre-weighted meter combines both ideas and gives an overall reading, but with more than 50% of the reading coming from the central area. A biased system will have a deliberate pattern designed to take more reading from the lower half of the screen so that bright skies on most photographs do not affect the settings.

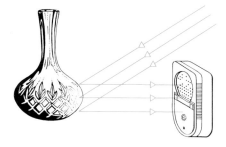

Two methods of using a hand meter: the top picture shows the meter reading the light reflected back from the subject as a TTL meter with this method, subjects of abnormal tonal quality must receive special consideration. An incident reading is taken from: light source itself (below).

Some systems have variable angle metering so that when the focal length of the lens changes, the pattern of centre-weighting changes too. With telephoto lenses, where the subject tends to fill the whole frame, the whole frame is integrated. With wide angles, which tend to have a lot of sky, only a narrow part of the scene in the centre is metered.

Hand held meters
Separate hand held meters have advantages for careful, serious photography. Many of them are able to meter narrow angles or have variable angles; most will measure both reflected and incident light, and some will measure both and take a combined reading. Some can measure flash. All are ideal for taking readings close-up to a subject without moving a camera positioned on a tripod. Spot meters cover approximately $1°$ and have separate viewfinders for accurate sighting. They are mainly used in cine work.

Built-in meters
Battery-operated meters are often built in to compact or 110 size cameras and linked to the shutter for auto or semi-auto exposure control. Usually they have no separate readout and cannot be used to read the light when setting any other camera. The angle of view of the meter is normally worked out to give a fair average success-rate ($20°$ is typical) and the meter window may be positioned very close to the lens so that any filters

A modern, hand held exposure meter with all its subtle calibrations.

or other accessories fitted will be compensated for in the reading.

TTL meters
With SLR much more accurate metering can be accomplished by siting the meter cells inside the optical system of the viewfinder, or even near the film itself. These systems read the actual light being passed through the camera lens and cope automatically with changes in angle of view, filters, close-up extensions, and so on. Instead of having calculator dials, TTL meters use the actual control scales of the camera, the f stops and shutter speed dial, so that these are adjusted to centre a needle or match up a small light array. As turning these settings also resets them, there is no possibility of 'taking a reading and forgetting to set the camera'. Metering with TTL is accurate and failsafe. Despite this, a hand held meter is often useful for close-up readings, which cannot be taken without moving the camera, or when you change to a telephoto lens.

Automatic metering
Either built-in or TTL meters may be coupled directly to the camera's controls, so that either one or both of the exposure settings is controlled by the meter directly, and does not have to be adjusted in any way by the user. Fully auto systems set both shutter and aperture and are not very versatile. Aperture priority systems allow the user to set the f stop, and then select the correct shutter speed (ideal for landscapes, architecture, general photographs) while shutter priority systems allow the user to pick the shutter speed and then select the f stop (ideal for sports, children, etc). Programmed systems have a range of preset combinations and are fully auto, but the user may be able to override them completely. The best automatic metering systems have override to adjust exposure without changing the ASA setting, or hold which enables the user to take a reading and lock the setting, many auto cameras have manual control too.

TTL meters indicate under- or over-exposure in a centring needle or a visual display.

Choosing the right camera

There are now so many cameras on the market that any would-be photographer could be forgiven for retiring baffled. The important thing is to decide what you want the camera for. For instance, if all you want is good holiday snaps which can be taken with the minimum of fuss. There is no point in buying an impressive machine that costs more than the holiday itself and takes twice as long to understand. Investigate the range of 'holiday snap' cameras and buy the best. It is better to err on the side of caution: you can always buy a more sophisticated camera next time.

Similarly, if you are thinking of taking up photography as a hobby, starting from scratch, it makes more sense to explore the limits of your enthusiasm and talent first on a good cheap camera, a 110 for example, before launching into the expensive end of the market, where the cost of the camera is nothing to the cost of its additional accessories.

Below is a guidance chart to help you choose the kind of camera you need to do the job you have in mind.

You want	You need
Cheap colour snaps in sunshine only, no loading, no settings.	'Disposable' type 110 camera pre-loaded with film
Small colour prints as above, but in dull light too.	Basic 110 camera, uses standard film in summer, 400 ASA film in dull light, flash indoors.
Good small colour prints in any light (recommended if you live in Northern latitudes, with changeable weather conditions.	110 camera with fast lens (f.5.6 or wider) and electronic exposure control.
Close-up shots, portraits, children and animals, flowers, etc.	110 camera with sliding close-up telephoto or zoom lens.
Pocketable camera but slides or prints up to 10 x 8 inches.	High quality 110 range-finder/auto exposure camera
Sharper, clearer prints in colour or b/w, good quality slides.	Compact 35mm camera with symbol focussing and auto exposure.
Same requirements but needing sharp close-ups, indoor groups, etc.	Compact 35mm fixed-lens rangefinder camera with auto exposure.
Camera to teach beginner basics of photography.	35mm model with manual settings (or manual override to auto exposure) and focussing.
Camera for easy loading without being too small for large hands.	Type 126 cartridge camera (restricted choice available, usually very basic).
Proper control over exact composition, focus, framing, viewpoint.	35mm camera with standard 50mm lens or a medium-range zoom lens of about 35–85 mm
Same requirements, but no controls to set except focus.	Fully auto SLR with no manual override.
Auto exposure most of the time but control when demanded/when you have mastered the techniques.	Fully auto SLR with manual override.
As above again, but with the option of a telephoto and wide-angle lens.	Nearly any 35mm SLR all have at least one tele-photo and wide-angle lens made.
Studio photography of people.	6 x 6cm SLR: Hasselblad, Bronica, Kowa, etc.
Same, but good choice of 2/3 telephotos, extreme wide-angle, close-up bellows.	35mm SLR with any one of following mount systems (ask your dealer): 42mm screw thread, Pentax K bayonet, Minolta bayonet, Kikon bayonet, Olympus bayonet, Konica bayonet, Canon breechlock, Mamiya bayonet, Leicaflex.
Same, but facility to have motorized film wind (just to save time).	Any SLR advertised as 'auto wind' or with 'auto winder' available.
Proper motor drive, sequences of rapid exposures and so on.	Not given by most auto winds, look for camera taking choice of winder or full motor drive at faster rate.
Weddings and portraits.	6 x 6cm SLR or TLR.
Instant colour prints.	Kodak, Polaroid, or other instant picture camera.
Instant colour prints, high standard of focus, framing, composition.	Polaroid SX-70 reflex or Kodak reflex.
Instant black and white prints.	Polaroid system only; check whether model you see will take black and white packs.
Instant black and white negatives.	Limited range of more expensive Polaroid types.
Pocketable 35mm camera.	Minox 35 EL, Rollei 35, or similar collapsing or folding type.
Camera for rugged industrial sites, dusty locations, shock resistant.	Cast-iron/alloy body 'press' camera: Koni-Omega, Mamiya Press (obsolete), Horseman Convertible, Sinar Handy, KLB GeePee.
Camera for panoramic views	Widelux or Panon scanning camera (normally restricted to tripod use); also Horizont (Russian, restricted availability).
Stereo (3-D) photography.	Stero beamsplitter attachment for your 35mm

Choosing the right film

Your first choice in film type will probably be based on the result you want. Colour slide film does not produce monochrome prints, and colour negative film will not make slides. Perhaps you need more than one end result—colour slides and prints, or colour and black and white prints. In this case, films can be versatile enough to cope, but costs are always higher and results inferior to using two cameras and two correct types of film.

Colour slides are suitable for projection, making small enprints (a service available widely from film manufacturers and colour processing labs), reproduction in books and magazines, photo contests for slides, reproduction on television, and making special but expensive prints to be displayed outdoors in direct sunlight. **Colour negatives** are suitable for inexpensive small prints, good quality enlargements at moderate cost, black and white prints of acceptable quality, reproduction in magazines, photo contests for prints, novelties (photo badges, table-mats, etc). **Black and white negatives** are suitable for all sizes and types of black and white print, black and white slides, reproduction in magazines and newspapers, all black and white photo contests, and novelties as above. They are also the ideal introduction to DIY processing and printing.

When choosing your film, you should also consider the following criteria. Black and white film can record the finest detail for copying documents. Colour negatives are the easiest form to have processed and printed in any part of the world and produce the most acceptable colour in mixed or unfamiliar lighting. On the other hand, slides are the cheapest form of photograph, and slide projection is the only adequate way of showing more than about six people a set of photographs. They also produce the most accurate colour in 'correct' lighting (i.e. daylight). However, duplicate slides are expensive and if several copies of a photograph are needed it is better to use colour prints or take what you want at the time.

Once you have selected the type of result you need, there are various types of film available in each category to suit different conditions of use. The most important variable

is *film speed*. This is the degree of sensitivity of the film to light, and is normally expressed in ANSI or ASA ratings. A 'standard' speed film today is normally considered to be 100 ASA, a sensitivity which allows an exposure of roughly 1/125 at f.16 in the brightest sunlight (temperate latitudes!). With most cameras this means that photographs can be taken under a wide range of conditions, including indoors by domestic light, and action photographs at 1/1000 of a second are possible on fairly dull days.

A speed of 25 ASA would, in exchange for needing four times the exposure, be much more finely detailed and sharp, with less grain and better colours or tones. A speed of 400 ASA allows action pictures even in the rain and good photographs in domestic lighting, needing only one-quarter of the standard exposure, but will be grainy and not very sharp, with inferior colours.

The other main variable, which applies only to colour film, is between daylight film and artificial (tungsten) light film: daylight film is balanced to give correct colours with the daylight spectrum; tungsten light bulbs, like photofloods or QI cine lights, are much yellower, and would give yellow-brown results on daylight film. So special tungsten light film is made in colour slide and negative forms to compensate. It is not essential to use this special material with colour negative, especially with the 400 ASA types, but it can help if exposures are longer than about 1/8 second. In colour slide film it is most valuable as no correction of the colours can be made afterwards.

The alternative to tungsten light film is a blue correction filter which cuts down the incoming light by half; as tungsten light is rarely very bright, this is the last thing which most photographers want to do.

When buying or taking it with you, always allow for the worst possible conditions. If you are shooting motor racing, take 400 ASA film rather than 25 ASA even if the sun is shining when you set off—or preferably take some of each. If the sun goes in or you are still shooting at dusk, the 400 ASA film will make results possible which the 25 ASA would not. If you are photographing buildings with a tripod, then the 25 ASA film would be quite acceptable—but a roll of 100 or 400 ASA in your pocket would help greatly if you arrive to find the building on fire and want some spontaneous action shots of the fire crew. If you are photographing a wedding, 100 ASA colour negative film would be an obvious choice as it gives pleasant results and colours and is easy to make prints for the guests. But if the wedding was in your own family and you wanted some different, more intimate pictures, 400 ASA slide film would allow pictures without flash in church (if permitted) and candlelight shots at the reception.

Fortunately all the three main types of film—black and white, colour negative and colour reversal—are available in the three main speeds, the exception being the lack of a very slow (25 ASA) colour negative film, as the 100 ASA types normally sold are detailed enough for even the most fastidious photographer.

Subject	Film suggested
Portraits, single and group	Kodak Vericolor or any other 100 ASA colour negative stock
Indoor colour slides: electric light	Kodak Ektachrome 160 Tungsten
Rock concerts, floodlit sports, circuses, theatre: fluorescent light	Kodacolour 400 balanced for mixed light, Ektachrome 400, Tri-X, Kodacolour 400
Landscapes	Kodachrome 64, Agfachrome 50S, FP4, 100 ASA colour negative stock
Seascapes	Kodachrome 25 or 64, FP4, Agfa CNSII
Architecture: exteriors	Kodachrome 25, Pan-F any 100 ASA
Animals (Zoos, parks)	Ektachrome 200, Tri-X, any 400 ASA colour negative stock.

How colour film works

Basically, colour film is three normal black and white films sandwiched together to form one multiple layer coating. Each layer has been modified to react only to the appropriate colour. One responds only to blue light, one to red, and one to yellow. The film, if it was developed normally in black and white developer, would look very much black and white. Colour developers have further chemical components which act on extra chemicals and dyes in the film layers to produce coloured dye in proportion to the image. The processing results in a colour picture, not a monochrome one.

There are various methods by which the black silver in the three film layers is turned into coloured dye. In most, the dye is generated in the film itself, using chemicals which are changed when silver compounds near them or linked to them are turned to silver. The change results in the formation of the colour. The black silver then has to be removed, as only the dye image is required, and this is done with a special bleach which does not affect the dyes. So although colour film depends on silver to begin with, the final result may have none in it, just the dye the silver helped to form.

Colour negatives

Colour negatives are even harder to 'read' than black and white ones, but work on exactly the same principle. Each colour in the spectrum has its 'complementary' colour, a colour which if added to it would create white light. Red's complementary colour is blue-green; blue's is yellow; green's is magenta. Colour negatives work by making each colour of light that falls on the film create not its own colour of dye but its complementary colour. The process can then be repeated using a printing paper with the same characteristics to recover the original colours.

The reason why a colour negative looks so very different, and is not made up of bright complementary colours, has to do with practice and not principle. Deficiencies in the dyes and chemicals, preventing the photographic scientists from making a simple colour negative as described, demand the use of further techniques. The colours produced are adjusted slightly. The background colour of the film is changed to bright orange, which is destroyed where there is image-detail, to allow the other colours to be picked out clearly. The sensitivity of the printing paper is adjusted to this unusual shade.

The end result is exactly as required although the route is different. A colour negative may not look like a true negative version of the scene, but as far as the paper is concerned they are. Modern colour films often use more than the three layers. Many use six. The development rate and exact sensitivity of each layer must be precise. Tolerances in colour film manufacture are reduced to the absolute minimum and processing is carried out to within a fraction of a degree. Each batch of film has to be individually assessed for printing and two negatives taken on one roll at different times may need different settings in the colour lab. This is very far removed from the black and white world, but as a result the colours obtained today are much purer and brighter than they could have been at their best ten years ago. The only way to learn how to judge and assess colour negatives and really understand how they work is to print your own.

Colour transparencies

In a black and white negative, the last important processing stage is the removal of the unexposed, undeveloped silver compounds which

A positive colour image as produced by a transparency or a print from negative.

A colour negative shows the dark tones as light and reverses colours.

would otherwise eventually turn black and spoil the film. These compounds exist in inverse proportion to the main image. Where the main image is very dense, there are hardly any unexposed grains, and where it is 'thin' there are many. This makes it possible to make black and white slides, using chemicals which remove the first (negative) silver image and then develop the remaining silver salts to form a positive image. This image is the exact reversal of the negative, made by using the materials which the negative has not already used up.

Exactly the same thing happens in colour transparency film. With its basic three layers, just like colour negative film, it produces a black and white image. The reversal processing sequence then colour-develops the residual unexposed emulsion, while the black silver images from the first development are destroyed and removed from the film. In colour reversal, the coloured dyes naturally match the original red, blue and yellow primaries of the scene. Unlike the cheaper colour negative material, tolerances in manufacture avoid the changes in colours which could happen between batches.

In transparency films, the maximum density of the three dye layers would be too weak, even at their darkest, to make a full black. So

some black silver is allowed to remain in the film as a positive image to back up the density of the dyes. This adds to the range of tones and colours possible and is one reason why colour slides look much 'stronger' than colour prints in many cases. An incorrectly developed slide may show green or magenta shadows because the dye-layers are not evenly developed and there is not enough density, silver or not, to block light off completely and create black.

Instant prints

Like both colour negative and colour reversal films, instant print films come from the black and white principle. The variety of processes is far greater than that in colour films of conventional camera type, because there is no need for compatibility in processing—the film does it itself.

The principles are identical in effect to colour reversal film, though a transparency is not the object. In instant print colour, the first negative image is produced by developing one layer using developing chemicals contained in the material or distributed over it automatically when the film is pulled out of the camera. The reversal image, the opposite of the negative image, is not formed in the same layer but *migrates*. It is transferred to another layer, where it combines chemi-

cally with built-in 'receptors' to fix in position and form colour dyes. The negative image and all the by-products of processing remain in the original negative layer, while the print you finally view, is permanent and free from contamination.

In peel-apart instant image processes, the negative half is discarded, as the image transfers from one sheet of material to an entirely separate sheet. In the transfer it also turns itself round physically as the images are face-to-face, so the final image is a mirror version of the negative. As the camera lens produces a mirror image translation initially, this results in a corrected image.

With dry, one-piece, instant image print film, the negative layer is concealed behind a chemical barrier which is formed during processing; this barrier is a brilliant white in colour to provide a background for the coloured dyes. In the Polaroid system the exposure is through the front of the film, using a camera with a mirror system which corrects the mirror image produced by the lens. In the Kodak system the image is exposed on the back of the film and migrates through to the front, and this performs the reversal of the mirror image. Both these systems use dyes unlike those in normal colour film and the colours have a distinct quality of their own.

Tungsten lighting used with daylight film has created an orange cast.

Daylight used with tungsten film has produced a blue cast.

Lenses

The reason why 35 mm SLR cameras have interchangeable lenses is to allow a change in the angle of view—that is, the amount of subject 'covered' by the camera at a given distance. A very wide angle of view, say 100°, would cover a whole room from a single corner—in fact it would include all four walls if the room was rectangular. A very narrow angle of view, such as 5°, would be equal to looking through a medium-power pair of binoculars.

Good lenses have a coverage which comfortably exceeds their intended angle of view. Poor lenses often work to the limits of their coverage, which begins to fall off in the corners of the picture. Because of design features, wide angle lenses have very good coverage, but it tends to fall off sharply. Telephoto lenses have very limited coverage, and although you would expect a very long telephoto like a 500 mm to be quite capable of working on both 35 mm and 6 × 6 cm formats, very few would do so satisfactorily.

Choosing a lens

Your 35 mm camera will probably have been supplied with a standard or compact standard lens, 50 mm or 40 mm. Choosing additional lenses is best done after trying out this standard and finding the kind of problems you have.

If your pictures are mainly of inanimate subjects like towns, buildings, room interiors, cars, landscapes, landmarks, and so on, a **wide angle lens** may be the best first choice, as it aids composition and enables many more viewpoints within a short distance of your subject.

Wide angles are also ideal for groups. If you are primarily interested in architecture, interiors, landscapes and townscapes, use a focal length of 24 mm; if you photograph people or use flash for many pictures, use 28 mm.

Some photographers prefer to take close-ups of people, to show emotions or simply make good portraits. If you want good close-ups and find your standard lens often leaves you too far away to do so, then a **telephoto** lens is the answer. The telephoto is also ideal for sports, natural history, animal photography, and some types of

View through 20 mm lens

View through 38 mm lens

View through 50 mm lens

24

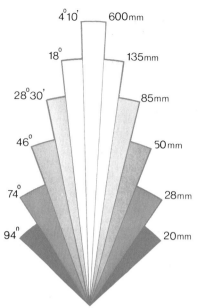

Focal length is the distance between the film and the lens. A long focal length gives a larger image size.

View through 85 mm lens

View through 135 mm lens

View through 600 mm lens

landscape photograph. It is also a more impressive lens in terms of the change in your pictures than a wide angle can prove to be. For people, especially indoors and with children, a lens of about 100 mm is ideal. For sports and outdoor photographs a 200 mm lens may be better. A popular compromise is the 135 mm telephoto, which is a good starting point. The best answer today is the **zoom lens**, and here the 70 to 150 mm type is best for children, whereas an 80 to 200 mm is good for outdoor work.

Expanding beyond the first wide angle and the first telephoto, the obvious second choice is to buy whichever type you don't buy first. The third lens you buy may pose a problem, but by this stage you will have a clearer idea of what you need from using the others. As a guide, avoid buying lenses too similar in focal length. The usual focal length ranges for 35 mm cameras are 17 mm, 20 mm, 24 mm, 28 mm, 35 mm, 40 mm, 50 mm, 85 mm, 100 mm, 135 mm, 200 mm, 300 mm, 400 mm, 500 mm, 1000 mm. If you pick your lenses by leaving a gap of one focal length between any two, you can't go far wrong.

The cheapest way to add a lens to your outfit is to buy a **telephoto converter**, a very compact optical tube which fits between camera and lens and doubles its focal length (it also quarters the amount of light transmitted). This turns a 50 mm into a 100 mm or a 135 mm into a 270 mm.

25

THE FOUNDATIONS OF PICTURE MAKING

Taking good pictures is largely a matter of observation, awareness and concentration. Observation is not just a question of simply looking at things, but really seeing them clearly and objectively. Awareness means analyzing what you see and understanding how and why what you are seeing makes you want to take a photograph. A little concentration is all you need to combine the results of your observation and awareness into a satisfying and effective photograph.

The eye and the camera

The camera lens has a very objective view of the world. It sees only what it is pointed at and it makes no allowances. In contrast, our eyes tend to ignore the unsavoury and exaggerate the favourable, and are affected by sounds, smells, memories and even our mood. During waking hours they are constantly working usually without conscious thought or effort, relaying a continuous flow of visual information from everything within range. The camera lens, on the other hand, records only a restricted view and has to be directed to specific scenes. It also 'sees' only in two dimensions in comparison to the binocular vision we enjoy.

This goes a long way to explain the sometimes disturbing differences between what you thought you saw and what the camera recorded when you examine your processed films. It is this difference which causes many of the problems from which inexperienced photographers suffer. The classic boobs like trees growing out of people's heads and buildings leaning over are some of the obvious symptoms of this problem, but even experienced photographers can have lapses of concentration.

The photographer's eye explains the difference between the two pictures of the Arab women leaning against a tree. The larger picture on the right represents what the untrained eye might see. The smaller picture shows just how much more may be in the field of view but is being subconsciously ignored. The camera of course will not ignore it, and all of the extraneous and unattractive details will be included in the picture.

Selecting the image

There can be a great deal of difference between what we are looking at and what we actually see. There is an amusing party game which underlines this. You show a number of people the same scene and ask them afterwards to describe what they saw. The differences can be quite staggering. Each tends to see only what interests or stimulates them, the remainder being suppressed by a personal system of mental selection. With the camera however, this selection process has to be done physically. By choosing the position and angle of the camera and using different lenses and accessories, parts of the scene which do not contribute to the picture can be excluded or subdued.

The essence of good photography is the ability to recognize the significant elements of something which arouses your interest and to know what is unnecessary or distracting. Sometimes you must be very ruthless, excluding everything but the main centre of interest; in other circumstances the effect of a picture can be greatly enhanced by including other objects. This ability and its acquisition is largely a matter of awareness combined with experience. Taking pictures from different positions and of different areas of a scene and then comparing the results is by far the most effective way of learning to be a good photographer. Developing a visual awareness is by no means as daunting as it may sound, and as soon as you begin looking and seeing in a conscious and positive way, taking good photographs becomes a matter of choice rather than chance.

What to leave out is a problem illustrated by these two pairs of pictures. The bicycles parked outside a bar in Copenhagen offered the photographer two possibilities at least. Some people will prefer one, and some the other. The answer is to shoot the alternatives where possible, unless you are really sure, and then to compare the results.

The lakeside scene in Italy offers a more positive choice. The top picture really has too much going on, and too much with not enough going on. In this instance, leaving something out and framing more tightly has resulted in a more effective picture. By excluding the large area of empty foreground and the rather fussy tangled branches of the trees on the right, the photographer has focussed attention on a more specific and dramatic element of the scene.

Colour awareness

Colour, like most things around us, tends to get taken for granted. If it is exceptional or unexpected, such as a dramatic sunset or a vivid pink car, it might raise a response, but on the whole it goes unnoticed. The photographer must learn to see the individual colours in the subjects he wants to photograph, to be aware of how they react with each other, to know if they contribute to the mood of the picture, and to see how they relate to the composition of the image. It is possible to have a photograph in which all of the other elements are in perfect balance with each other, but the end result has been completely destroyed by the wrong or inappropriate use of colour. A bit like wearing a red tie at a funeral.

Colour should not be thought of as a separate element that must be treated in a different way to shape, form, contrast, tone, texture and other components. It should be simply considered and incorporated into the picture as part of the overall composition. The problem is, however, that colour tends to be rather

more overwhelming and emotive than the other elements and, unless care and control is exercised, colour content can easily dominate.

There is a series of stages of awareness that can easily be applied to the colour quality of any subject. The first is to know what is the overall colour impression. It may be green in a summer landscape, for example, or brown in an autumn woodland scene or simply the flesh colour in a portrait. The next stage is to be aware of the colours in the subject that comprise this overall effect. The green landscape for example may also contain brown, yellow and blue. Then you must see how these colours relate to each other. Do they create contrast or do they harmonize? If there is a contrasting colour, does it contribute to the composition or does it detract from it? It is vital to ask yourself these questions because it is not until you are aware of the answers that you can begin to see the image in terms of a colour photograph, as opposed to a photograph with colours in it.

Many experienced photographers find it difficult to switch quickly from shooting black and white to shooting colour on the same assignment. This is because taking a picture in colour involves a mental readjustment to accommodate the rather powerful element of colour into making of the image. It is also true that a black and white print made from a good colour picture is unlikely to produce an aesthetically satisfying result, because an important ingredient has been removed.

A riot of colour would be a fair description of this picture taken in an Arab bazaar. Although almost irresistable to the novice with a camera loaded with colour, it does not prove to be a very satisfying colour picture. There is simply too much going on. Each colour fights its neighbour and none of them really win. It is necessary to look very carefully at the colours in a picture, what they are, where they are and what they do to each other, before you begin.

A good colour photograph is an equally fair description of this shot of fishing boats on the beach at Nazaré in Portugal. There are still bright colours in the scene but they don't fight each other, the eye is led through the picture by the arrangement of colours and shapes and the result is a pleasing and satisfying image.

COMPONENTS OF AN IMAGE

All photographs, no matter what their subject matter, are made up from the same basic ingredients. Whether it is a herd of stampeding elephants or a still life of a vase of flowers, it can be analyzed and considered in the same way.

Shape

The basic ingredient in most photographs is the shape (or shapes) that they contain. Many things can be identified by their shape, or outline, alone whereas others need further information to be sure. There would be little doubt, for example, if one saw a giraffe silhouetted against the sky, whereas the shape alone of, say, a fox could be confusing. An isolated shape can provide an interesting image. A dark object silhouetted against the sky, a window or a white wall or a light coloured object against a dark background need be all that is necessary to make a satisfying photograph. You should train yourself to look for pictures like this as part of your self-conducted visual awareness programme.

It is the outline of the subject which is the most dominant element of this photograph. Everything else is lost or subdued and the interest of this image depends almost entirely on its shape.

Form

If shape is the bones of an image, then form is the flesh. The outline of a round object tells us little about it. It may be simply a disc, a sphere or the end of a cylinder: it is only when you see its form that you can identify it correctly.

It is the ability of the photographic process to record subtle gradations of tone that enables it to convey the impression of form. This in turn is largely responsible for the convincing illusion of reality that photographs convey. In a good photograph, the squareness of a box or the roundness of a ball can be felt by the viewer almost as strongly as if it were the real thing. Photographs which fully exploit the quality of form convey the greatest impression of reality. This aspect of photography is expressed vividly in the sensuous still-life and landscapes of Edward Weston.

Light is, of course, essential to all photography, but it is the very subtle interplay of light and form that is the real essence of most good pictures. It is the almost magical ability of the photographic process to record this response which greatly contributes to the illusion of depth that can be created in a two dimensional photograph.

Because it is so vital for a photographer to be fully aware of this interplay in the subjects he photographs, it is perhaps the first thing to be considered when deciding how it should be photographed. Pictures which do not take full advantage of this quality can, of course, still be successful images, but they will depend much more on the design and interplay of the shapes within the photograph.

Texture

Form tells us what an object would be like to hold; texture tells us what it would be like to touch. Form is to do with the body of an object but texture is the nature of its surface. One of the unique qualities of photography is its ability to portray textures very realistically. A good photograph of, say, an egg laying on a piece of silk should let you almost

32

The quality of form is most pronounced in this picture of rocks. It conveys an almost tangible feeling of solidity and reality. It is this element which is most dominant and which has created the effect of this photograph.

feel the differences in the surfaces.

A picture which utilizes the quality of texture tends to bring a photograph ever closer towards reality. This is not always desirable, and it is interesting to see that when an unreal or romantic effect is wanted, techniques such as soft focus are introduced which often destroy the textural quality of the image. For example, you rarely see the texture of female skin in a photograph for a cosmetic ad, but in a cigarette advertisement where a realistic rugged male is depicted you can see every bristle in his five o'clock shadow. The quality of texture can be a powerful ingredient in a picture when it is used appropriately.

You can almost feel the rough texture of this old man's skin. The ability to convey the visual quality of a surface vividly and accurately is one of the most powerful elements in the photographic process. When used in this way, it is an invaluable means of creating a sense of realism in an image. A picture like this should be as sharp as it can be.

Pattern

Pattern is the repetition of shapes within a picture. It can exist in something perfectly regular like a stack of bricks and also in something quite irregular like ripples on the surface of water. It can easily be a very dominant force in a picture and should be used with discretion: a picture which consists only of a pattern may be initially compelling, but it is unlikely to have a lasting appeal. Nevertheless, a picture which has an element of pattern tends to be rather pleasing to the eye and imparts a feeling of re-assurance and harmony.

Perspective

Perspective is one of the most important qualities in any of the graphic arts as it is one of the elements which enables a two dimensional image to give the impression of being three dimensional. It works

The element of pattern in this picture is part of a composition but it is the repetition of the shapes in this image which makes an interesting photograph from a commonplace scene.

on the principle that objects of the same size seem progressively smaller the further they are away from the observer. Two similar houses side by side will appear to be the same size, but if one of the houses is 100 metres behind the other it will appear to be substantially smaller. If you know that it is really the same size, then you also know that it is further away. The opposite is, of course, equally true. A small object seen close to will appear to be the same size as a large one at a greater distance. All of this may seem very obvious but it is surprising how many unsuccessful photographs are produced because someone has not been sufficiently aware of this elementary fact. Everyone has taken a picture of a person standing in front of a distant building, and yet when the resulting photograph is seen, the building has become almost lost in the distance. This is because the eye adjusts, zooming in on the distant object whilst keeping the foreground in view. The camera, of course, simply cannot do this and it is essential to

train yourself into constant awareness of the relationship between the apparent size of the objects in the scene you want to photograph.

The diminishing size of progressively more distant objects also creates another quality within the image which is important to understand. This is the creation of lines travelling away from the edges of the picture and converging to a point in the distance. You can easily grasp this if you stand in the centre of a road. The edges will then appear to converge until they meet at a point in the centre of the horizon. This is known as the vanishing point and when these perspective lines are strong in a picture the eye will always be led towards this point. These lines and where they converge are very important factors to consider when it comes to composing a picture.

Perspective and converging lines have created quite a dramatic image from a row of abandoned park deckchairs. Again a relatively mundane scene has been given a pictorial quality by one particular element of photographic composition.

Tone

Tone is the transition of light to dark within the image. It is the ability of the photographic process to record the subtleties of this transition that make possible the tremendous range of effects attainable in a photograph. The distribution of tone is probably the single most important factor in deciding the nature and quality of a photograph. A picture consisting of only solid black and pure white would do little more than indicate the basic shapes or outlines of the objects within it. As other tones are introduced, other qualities are revealed. Form and texture are almost totally dependent on the tonal range of the subject. It is as necessary for the photographer to become as aware of the distribution of light and shadow, and all the subtleties in between, as it is for a painter.

Apart from the ability of tone to record the quality of the image, it is also an important factor in setting the mood of a picture. A picture which consists primarily of darker tones will invariably be of a sombre nature, while a picture containing only the lighter tones in the range will have a delicate, ethereal quality. A picture where bright tones and rich dark tones are interspersed will have a bold assertive quality, whereas one consisting of tones mostly from the middle range will tend to be quiet and restful.

High key is the term used to describe images like the one above of trees reflected in a pond. This picture consists primarily of tones from the lighter areas of the scale. A misty day has softened the daylight and reduced the tonal range quite dramatically. This type of photograph requires full exposure, often even slight overexposure.

Low key treatment has been given to this picture of Hastings Pier, Sussex. Shooting into a low, late afternoon winter sun has created a fairly high contrast image. Using an exposure calculated to render the highlight areas as a mid tone has resulted in a picture consisting primarily of tones from the darker areas of the scale. With this type of subject, you should give less than the normal calculated exposure and ensure that there is adequate highlight detail in most areas of the subject.

A full range of tones has enhanced the dramatic quality of the picture of a windmill on the right. This image has made use of every tone, from white to black, that the process is capable of recording. Precise exposure is needed to ensure that detail is recorded in both the brightest highlights and all but the densest shadows.

36

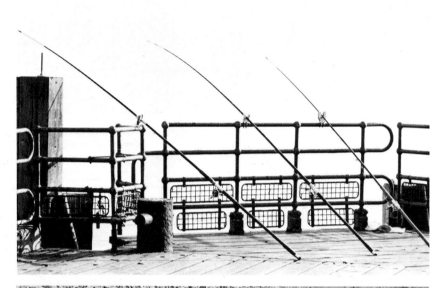

A high contrast subject like fishing rods leaning against a railing (top) is dependent on the use of tones at opposite ends of the range. In this case there are few intermediate tones and the result is a near silhouette.

Low contrast in a picture happens when there is only a limited range of tones, as in this photograph of an old man sitting in the shade. The soft light obtained in open shade does nothing to increase the contrast of an inherently soft or low contrast subject. If the old man had been wearing black, it would have resulted in a picture of a more normal tonal range. A similar effect would have been achieved if the subject had been lit by a harder light, direct sunlight for example.

Contrast

The difference in brightness between the strongest highlight in a photograph and the darkest shadow is called contrast. A great difference will result in a harsh or hard effect and a small difference will give a gentle or soft picture. A simple example would be a black cat photographed against a white wall and a grey cat against a grey wall. Extremes of contrast are usually undesirable. Photographic film simply cannot cope with a very wide range of brightness: lighter tones would be burned out and devoid of detail, and the darker tones completely lost in blackness. A picture with a very low brightness range can easily look muddy and dull. This is another situation where the eyes can be misleading. They can adjust swiftly from light to dark conditions, consequently evening out extremes of contrast. A useful trick is to view the subject through half-closed eyes, which will give you a much more accurate impression of the brightness range. If you plan to photograph someone indoors standing against a window, you might think that both the view through the window and the model's face could be recorded, but by looking through half-closed eyes you would probably find that you would in fact achieve only a silhouette.

Depth

The ability of a photograph, which is two dimensional, to imply the existence of the third dimension is dependent on the quality of depth. A feeling of depth can be created by a number of factors. The most important and obvious one is perspective but there are others which can help with this illusion. Tonal range can be a useful method of creating depth. Dark tones in the foreground of a picture and progressively lighter tones in the middle ground and distance greatly enhance the impression of depth. Landscape photographs which, by their nature, are usually of distant subjects are often improved by the deliberate inclusion of a closer, dark toned foreground such as a tree or a rock.

Using the tonal range to create modelling or form will also provide a sense of depth. A portrait or a nude in which the contours are 'modelled' by a rich range of tones can look positively three dimensional.

Contrast also can contribute to the illusion of depth. A dark object against a light background will appear to come forward towards the viewer. If you are using colour remember that red has a similar dominating effect whereas blue will appear to recede. As you gradually learn to assess the influence of these factors, you will be able to make them work together effectively.

Receding tones as in this woodland picture help to create a feeling of depth. A dark foreground gradually becomes lighter in the middle distance with the lightest tones in the far distance. This picture also has a strong element of perspective with very close foreground detail, which has been accentuated by using a wide angle lens.

THE QUALITY OF LIGHT

Light is, of course, essential to photography, but the mere existence of light does not guarantee a good picture. It is the quality of light which is one of the key factors determining the nature of an image. The constantly changing relationship between the light and the subject provides one of the greatest pleasures of photography and an awareness and understanding of this relationship is vital to the production of good pictures.

High summer sunlight provided the illumination for the picture of two Moroccan children (above). From directly overhead with a clear blue sky it has made quite strong but small shadows and created a boldly defined image with quite a high contrast. The effect of this harsh light has been mellowed by the reflective quality of the light coloured rock on which the children are standing, as it bounces light back into the dense shadows.

Low autumn sunlight has created long shadows in this picture taken in early morning in the Champs Elysées in Paris. This picture and the shot of the Moroccan children represent the two extremes of sunlight as far as angle and quality are concerned. In colour content, this picture would be warm and mellow and the other hard and bluish.

Hazy sunlight has given an image of equal brilliance in picture of a girl and a cow taken in Israel, but there are almost imperceptible shadows. A thin layer of atmospheric haze has acted like a diffusion screen over the hard sunlight retaining its brightness but scattering the light so that the shadows have received almost as much light. The sun in this scene was still a brilliant source of light but the sky itself was slightly milky. For many kinds of picture, this type of light is preferable to that of clear sun as there are no dense shadows to create problems.

40

Daylight
Daylight is the most commonly used light source in photography. It comes directly or indirectly from the sun, but can vary dramatically in quantity, quality, direction and colour, depending upon time of day, season of the year, geographical location and, of course, weather conditions.

An understanding of how and why it varies and what effects this can have on a photograph is vital for the photographer.

Direct sunlight
You might well imagine that direct light from the sun is pretty much the same the world over, since it has travelled billions of miles to get here and the world is relatively very small. This, however, is not true. There are many factors, each of which can have a marked effect on the quality of direct sunlight. The position of the sun in the sky is probably the most obvious of these, and the easiest to understand.

When the sun is directly over-head, the shadows it casts will be at their shortest and densest and the sunlight is least affected by the atmosphere. Of course, the direct overhead position occurs only at brief moments and in specific places. As the sun moves away from its zenith the shadows lengthen and change direction. This happens earlier or later in the day, according to the seasons and where you are in relation to the equator.

Think of the sun as a huge spot-light that travels in an arc over your subject. It cannot be directly controlled but an awareness of where it is and what it is doing can certainly help you make the most of it. You may still hear the advice 'Keep it (the sun) over your left shoulder and you'll be alright'. That's true to a point. If you take pictures un-thinkingly, you're more likely to have a lower incidence of total failure if you follow this advice, but its a bit like staying in bed to avoid traffic accidents—you're going to miss a lot of fun.

Being aware is a phrase that will crop up a great deal in this book and being aware of where the sun is, in which direction it is travelling and what effect its shadows are having, is the first step to making the most effective use of daylight. Of all the skills that a photographer needs, a knowledge of light and the effect it has is the most readily and most simply acquired.

Sky and clouds

Even on a cloudless day, the sky, or the atmosphere, can have a marked effect on sunlight. Industrial smog and moisture are two of the most common influences and their effect will be more prominent the closer the sun is to the horizon, as its beams have to travel further through the atmospheric layer. The most important result is slight softening of the sunlight. Shadows will begin to have a slightly diffused edge and they will not be so solid. The denser the atmospheric layer the more marked the effect, until the shadows are almost indiscernible although the sun is still visible in the sky.

Cloud, of course, has a much more dramatic effect. Even a small cloud can totally obscure the direct light from the sun. It is then that the sky itself becomes the source of light giving a completely different effect to that of sunlight. When dense cloud has completely covered the sky, the result will be a very soft light with no discernible shadows. This will give you a very low contrast range with no bright highlights and few very dark tones. Where only some cloud is present, together with blue sky, a certain brightness will be retained in the highlights, but as the cloud acts as a reflector, the shadow areas will be softened even when the sun is unobscured.

Smoke and steam have softened the strong sunlight of a summer's day in this shot of a steam engine. This effect is in a very limited area, but industrial haze and smoke can create a similar effect over hundreds of square miles in some areas, and has just as a dramatic effect on the sunlight as atmospheric conditions.

Autumn mist has created a very soft source of illumination in this woodland scene. There are many ways in which the light from the sun can be affected by local conditions, a mile or so away or a hundred metres or so higher up and the sunlight used in this shot would be unobscured and quite hard. It is important to realize that the quality of light can be greatly affected not only by the atmosphere but by local conditions as well. The light which you see from the window of your home may be very different from the light in the next town.

Hard and soft light

The lighting terms 'hard' and 'soft' refer to the nature of the shadows which are cast.

Hard light is that given by strong, direct sunlight which comes from a sun high in the sky. On a cloudless day the shadows will be sharply defined and very dense. In addition, highlights formed on glass and water and even glossy foliage will be brilliant, creating a very high contrast range.

Soft light, on the other hand, is that created when cloud or mist obscures the direct light of the sun. Shadows have only diffused edges and lack density and highlights are muted, resulting in tones of average contrast.

Very heavy cloud which completely covers the sky can result in flat lighting with no detectable shadows and virtually no highlights, thus producing a very low brightness range.

Recognizing light effects

It is of course the *effect* of light rather than the light itself that mostly concerns photographers and it can be very informative to start looking at objects under different lighting conditions to see the effect created. Choose one familiar object, like a building which you pass every day, as a reference point, and make a point of observing it under as many different lights as possible —daylight, tungsten, bright sunlight, overcast conditions, rain and so forth. This will help you sharpen your awareness of the effects of light.

Hard light from a brilliant, unobscured sun has created a very contrasting image of this seaside pavilion. The shadows are dense and have a hard, sharply defined edge. This type of lighting needs to be used with care. The slightest change of viewpoint will dramatically alter its effect. In portraiture, for example, light of this quality can create ugly shadows and create images of unmanageable contrast range.

A very soft light has been produced by a dense layer of cloud in this picture of rugby-playing children. There are virtually no shadows and the contrast range of the image is dependent on the subject itself; the lighting has done nothing to increase it. This type of lighting enables the photographer to shoot from almost any angle with no significant change in the lighting effect. It is ideal for subjects which are moving or where the photographer needs to change his viewpoint, because there are no dense shadows to create problems.

43

Light and form

Form is the most crucial element in a picture which is controlled almost solely by the nature of the lighting. The right light can almost bring an object to life and the wrong one can destroy it. It is at this point that you must consider the direction of the light in relation to your subject.

If you position a white sphere on a black background so that the sun shines directly onto the front of it, you would see only a white circle as there would be no shadows formed within the area of the sphere itself. You would in fact see its outline perfectly, but not its form. If you then change the position of the sphere so that the sun is at an angle to the side, a shadow would be created on the further side, and the form would begin to emerge. However, as a hard source of light (the sun) is being used, the transition of highlight to shadow

would be very sudden, resulting in part of the sphere being white and the rest nearly black. It will still not look like a sphere. Observe the phases of the moon for a perfect demonstration of this effect. However, if the sunlight were softened by a thin cloud or even a piece of tracing paper placed near to the sphere the transition from highlight to shadow would become much more gradual, producing a range of tones from white through light and darker greys to near black on the furthest side. This would create a much stronger impression of a sphere. An even stronger effect could be achieved by moving the sphere so that the light source was directed at an angle of almost 90°, creating a strong modelling on that side of the sphere but leaving the further side in deep shadow. If you now place a reflector such as a piece

of white card or polystyrene near the darker side you will create a secondary reflected light source, relieving the dark shadow and introducing a further tonal range

Using a reflector to 'fill in' shadow areas which are darker than required is an invaluable area of control for the photographer. The more pronounced or indented the contours of the subject are then the less acute is the angle of the light source required to reveal them, as the shadows formed are more pronounced themselves. The opposite, of course, is equally true. As contours become subtler, an increasingly acute angle of lighting is needed. Using a softened light source at an angle to the side, above or even below an object with a reflector if necessary, is most likely to reveal form in the subject and produce a pleasing image.

Backlighting reveals nothing but the basic shape of the subject. The result is virtually a silhouette, and while the image is perfectly recognizable the amount of visual information is quite limited and much is left to the viewer's imagination. This type of lighting tells us nothing at all about the form of a subject and very little indeed about its surface.

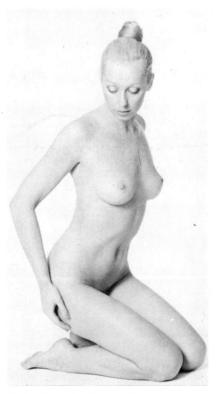

Light from the front tells us much more about the subject than the backlighting revealed. Although the outline is not so boldly displayed, it is still quite clear, and details in the skin, face and hair of the model are now quite easily seen. There are a few soft shadows on the body, but there is still very little impression of form. The body has no depth and there is no sense of solidity. Like the first picture, it is essentially a two dimensional image.

A directional light above and right has created a definite impression of solidity. This lighting reveals the form of the body. Strong shadows have been created and there is a much greater range of tones in the image. This quite strongly directional light from the left has, however, created large areas of dark shadow with no detail. A secondary light source has created further tones in the shadow areas.

Texture and pattern

Light and texture

Texture is another element of the image which is heavily dependent on the right lighting. Like form, texture is most likely to be revealed with a strongly directional light source. In many cases where the texture is quite subtle, an undiffused direct light can be even more effective than a soft source. Oiled and gleaming suntanned brown skin, for instance, can look amazingly realistic when lit with the harsh hard light of the unobscured sun. But do remember that the light required for the strongest rendition of texture may be less than desirable for the other elements of the subject. In fashion photography, for example, hard directional lighting is rarely used since although it would reveal the texture of the fabrics, it would do little to enhance the form and shape of the garments let alone the faces of the models.

Low hard sunlight has created this strong textured image of Victorian ironwork. It was taken in late afternoon in autumn, when the sun is at its lowest, creating a beautiful light.

Lighting for texture often needs to be quite hard and strongly directional, as demonstrated in these two studio still-life pictures. The picture above has been lit quite conventionally with a soft reflector on the flash which was used from a position a metre to the right of and slightly above the camera position. The picture on the right was lit with direct flash at table-top level and at right angles to the camera position. A white reflector and small mirror were used on the left hand side of the picture to lighten up the shadows and to add a small highlight to the apple.

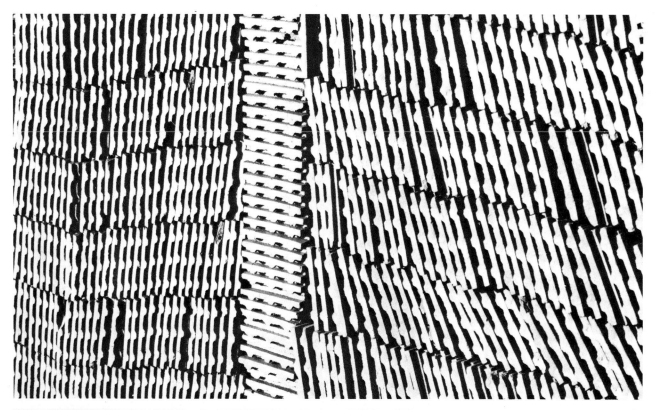

Light and pattern

It is impossible to make hard and fast rules about the best light required to reveal pattern in the subject. Some patterns exist simply because of the shapes of the objects within it. In these cases it could well be that anything but a soft, frontal, non-directional light might destroy the pattern by introducing shadows which confuse the image. On the other hand there are many circumstances where a pattern is created entirely by the shadows which a hard directional light might introduce. It is a useful exercise to look out for temporary patterns produced this way.

An inherent pattern exists with subjects like this stack of tiles, whatever the nature of the lighting. In this picture, the light was strong sunlight which has made the shadows quite dense, but even on a cloudy day a very similar effect would be created, although not quite so defined. The tonal range is limited, there is little impression of form or depth and the result is an image with a graphic quality.

Lighting can create pattern as in this picture of a backlit gate. The long shadows created by a low sun have become the dominant element. On a dull day, or even when the sun was high in the sky, there would be no pattern. This photograph relies on a full range of tones and a feeling of depth. There is also a quality of texture which contributes to the overall effect.

Light for landscapes

Landscape photography is the one area of photography where you are at the complete mercy of the light. After all, you cannot pick up a landscape and move it around until the light is at the right angle. If the light is not suitable for a landscape photograph there is little to do other than wait until it is, or forget it. But what is the right light for landscape? It is simply the light that reveals those qualities which you find stimulating in a particular scene. It may be the soft, gentle light of dusk or early morning for a tranquil lake view in the mountains, or the harsh, dry midday sun in a desert landscape. What can be so exciting in landscape photography is a sudden change in the lighting conditions which can reveal a dramatic picture in what had previously been an uninspiring scene. Likewise an exciting picture can just as quickly disappear. There is an immediacy and spontaneity in landscape photography as great as that in sport or reportage photography.

Many landscape photographers prefer to work in the early morning or late afternoon when the sun is lower in the sky, providing a more directional light with longer shadows and more pronounced contours. Often a landscape with very gentle contours can become more of an exercise in texture than form and the best light may well be quite hard as well as strongly directional. On the other hand, in mountain terrain for example, the contours can be so pronounced that such lighting would produce large areas of unintelligible black shadows.

In normal circumstances, a very dull overcast day may well be considered unsuitable for landscape photography, but sometimes the subtle and limited range of tones dictated by these conditions can produce images of great beauty. Fog, mist and rain can also create lighting conditions which transform an otherwise boring view into an unusual and dramatic picture. It may well prove to be a pleasant and surprising experience to venture forth with a camera on a dull, misty, rainy day and explore the photographic potential of bad weather.

An overcast day with very soft light was responsible for the bleak quality of this picture of Ebbw Vale in South Wales. The lighting is virtually shadowless. Without the strong shapes and texture of the mill wheels in the foreground there would be little or no impression of depth. The distant hillside with the matchbox terraced cottages appears as flat as a painted canvas backdrop, but it is the juxtaposition of the bold foreground and the flat grey background which makes it a successful photograph.

Low evening sunlight skimming over the Moroccan landscape (below left) has created a totally different image, rich in texture with strongly modelled contours. This almost sensuous quality is totally dependent on the nature and direction of the light: it would not have existed at midday when the sun was high in the sky. At this time of the day the effect of the light can change swiftly and dramatically.

Early morning mist combined with backlighting has created the ghostly tree-lined avenue below. The mist has simplified the image, reducing both the distant detail and the tonal range. Inspite of the perspective effect there is little impression of depth and virtually no texture or form. It is a picture primarily dependent on the quality of the light and the shape of the subject. An extra touch of drama has been created by using a wide angle lens, shooting from a low viewpoint and tilting the camera upwards.

A cloudy day in England's lake district gives a soft muted quality in this picture of Ennerdale Water. A small patch of weak sunlight filtered through the cloud to create an area of highlight in the middle distance without which the picture would be rather flat. On a day when there is a fair amount of cloud, small localized areas of sunlight can result in very pleasing lighting effects for landscape photography. This picture was shot on a long lens and the distant viewpoint has enhanced the scale of the far off mountain, increasing its dramatic quality.

High noon sunlight has created a fairly harsh quality in this picture of the Andalucian village of Casares. This type of landscape and architecture seem meant to be seen in this type of light, and the inclusion of the brightly coloured flowers in the foreground accent the whiteness of the houses and the blue sky. The picture was shot on a wide angle lens to allow the inclusion of close foreground details. Kodachrome 25 film was used which seems particularly suited to bright sunlight conditions.

Soft afternoon sunlight was used in this simple spring landscape shot in southern England. Although opposite in almost every way to the picture above, the light seems equally appropriate to the type of landscape. A polarizing filter was used to add a little colour to a rather pale English blue sky and the picture was shot on a long lens to isolate a fairly small area of the scene. The distant viewpoint helps to create a picture with a very slight impression of depth and perspective giving it a graphic quality.

Hazy sunlight has created an almost luminous quality in this monochromatic Dutch landscape. Simplicity is the keynote of this picture and bright sunlight and strong shadows, ripples on the water or the introduction of other colours would have completely destroyed its still, peaceful quality. A bright hazy sky can easily give a misleading exposure reading. Take the reading in a way that excludes most of the light from the sky, otherwise underexposure will result.

Light for portrait

When photographing people in daylight, you have a great deal more control than in landscape work, simply because the model can be moved around to suit the light. In this way, light can be directed a full 360° around the subject and, if necessary, the subject can be moved to another location where the lighting conditions are completely different. Every day, thousands of bad pictures are taken simply because the photographer has just raised his camera and pressed the button without even considering the fact that a slight move to one side or the other could make all the difference in the world to the lighting.

Lighting in portraiture has a great deal to do with the person you are photographing and the effect you want to achieve. A picture of a young girl, for example, may well look more pleasing if the lighting is soft and fairly frontal, avoiding strong modelling of the features. On the other hand, a portrait of an older person, where the essence may be the character and lines of the face, would require a rather harder directional light to accentuate these qualities.

Pictures taken with strong sunlight falling directly onto the face should generally be avoided for several reasons. First of all, it is uncomfortable for the model, causing squinting and other unsightly contortions. It also creates strong, dense shadows which are unflattering and unpleasing. Even on a sunny day it is easy enough to find small areas of shade adequate for a portrait. Alternatively, you can shoot with the sun behind the model. Providing the surroundings are light enough to reflect back into the face, or you use a reflector card, this can be very attractive.

Another way to avoid strong direct sunlight is to diffuse it with a large sheet of tracing paper or any white translucent fabric fairly close to the model. Fashion and beauty photographers often use this technique on outside locations and it can be very effective.

It must not be implied that one should *never* shoot with direct sunlight on the face, but it should be treated with great care. The strong shadows can be relieved by the use of reflectors or the face can be angled in such a way as to make the shadows more acceptable. The background and surroundings can also complement such a picture. A blue sea or sky, for example, behind a tanned, sunlit face will look more pleasing than a harshly-lit white face against a brick wall.

When preparing to take pictures of faces or people look at the alternative ways of lighting them before you start shooting. Not only will this avoid disappointments, but it will greatly increase your awareness and experience. Thus you will produce a more satisfying result.

Soft directional light has created a strongly modelled effect on the faces of these Neopolitan children photographed in a narrow street. Blocked on both sides by buildings, the light is coming mostly from above creating a quite rich range of tones. Even in diffused light, in shade or on a cloudy day it is important to be aware of the light's direction and of the shadows it creates. Often on a cloudy day the light can be too strongly directed from above causing unpleasant modelling. In these conditions it can be an improvement to position your model in a doorway.

Direct sunlight as used in this picture of a Moroccan shepherd on the left has created a strongly textured effect on his dark skin. In this instance it contributes to the quality of the picture, but this type of lighting should be used warily for portraits, since such exaggerated skin texture is often quite undesirable. On a light-skinned face, the dense shadows created by strong sunlight can be quite unpleasant.

Shooting against the light is an effective way of avoiding harsh shadows and squinting eyes when filming in sunlight. It can also isolate the subject clearly from the background and subdue unwanted detail (left). Remember that with this lighting exposure must be calculated so that faces are recorded as light tones. A close-up reading is the best method, making sure you exclude direct sunlight from the meter.

Open shade is another method of avoiding strong shadows on the face in outdoor portraits. Although this picture of Portuguese fishermen was taken on a sunny day, they were sitting in the shade of a building. The resulting lighting is virtually shadowless. This type of soft lighting is particularly suitable for groups of people when the faces occupy a small area of the picture and shadows can easily obscure them.

Light and colour

The effect of light on colour content can be seen in several different ways. The first has to do with the colour quality of the light source itself. As far as most manufacturers of film are concerned, there are two basic sources of light—daylight and tungsten. Colour films are balanced to suit one or the other. Daylight, however, varies greatly in colour quality. Daylight colour film is manufactured to give optimum results under very specific conditions and any variation in these conditions will produce a change in the colour quality of the result. Early morning or late afternoon sunlight for example has much more yellow content than noon sunlight and will give a warmer result if not corrected by filtration. A cloudy day, on the other hand, tends to produce light with more blue than that of midday sun. We usually don't notice slight changes such as these, but the colour film will record them quite faithfully. The eyes even adjust to drastic changes in the colour quality of the light source. We will still see

a piece of white paper as white, because we know it is white, even when it is lit by the relatively orange glow of tungsten light. Daylight colour film, however will see it as orange and it is only by using the correctly adjusted or balanced film (or correction filters) that it will appear as white on the film.

Although it is not too easy, it is possible to train your eye to see all but the slightest shifts in the colour of light. It is also possible, and easier, to buy a piece of equipment called a colour temperature meter, which measures shifts in colour quality. This is quite expensive, however, and not really necessary for all but the most accurate work. Filters can be used to correct variations in colour temperature but quite often the colour quality of the light can contribute to the effect of a picture rather than detract from it.

Pictures taken in late afternoon or early evening, for example, often owe a great deal of their mood to the warmth of the sunlight at this time of day. As a general rule pictures look quite attractive when the colour

quality of the light tends slightly to warm (orange), but can look distinctly less so when the light is excessively blue as on a cloudy day or in mountains or snow where there is a great deal of ultra violet light. Skin tones in particular can look quite unpleasant if they have a blue tinge and it is best to correct the balance in these circumstances.

It is not only the colour temperature of the light which has to be considered in colour photography but also the quality. Inexperienced photographers often think that bright sunlight is essential for bright colours, but this is not always so and in many circumstances can detract from the effect of a colour photograph. This is particularly true of objects that are brightly coloured themselves. A soft light from an overcast sky can often give them extra power and luminosity. A picture of a pile of fruit on a market stall for example may well be diminished by the highlights and shadows created by bright sunlight, whereas a soft light would allow the depth and intensity of their colours to come through. Advertising photographers shooting brightly coloured subjects prefer to work with a soft light for this reason.

No filter was used to create the orange glow in this picture, it was simply lit by the rays of a late afternoon sun in autumn, which shows just how yellow sunlight can be. In this case, the colour quality was considered to enhance the mood of the picture but it could have been moderated by the use of a correction filter. In general, flesh tones are quite pleasing when they have a warm cast but tend to be less pleasing if they have a blue or green cast.

Dull overcast daylight was used to photograph this floating grocers shop in Venice. This type of lighting is often preferable where there are bright colours present. Full sunlight can detract from such a picture. It is important not to over-expose this type of image as to do so would weaken the colours, in fact a slight degree of underexposure is often preferable. A long lens was used to isolate a small area of the scene and restrict the number of colours present in the image, thereby increasing their impact.

The mixed lighting in this pavement café scene in Paris clearly shows the way that colour film responds to changes in the colour quality of light. Taken at dusk, the area lit by the remaining daylight has a distinctly blue tinge while the interior of the café, lit by tungsten lighting, is a bright orange. This picture has used these effects consciously.

The blue quality of this picture taken just after the sun had gone down shows the Mersey ferry leaving the jetty in Liverpool in melancholy mood. A few minutes earlier showed an entirely different effect, as the setting sun gave a warm yellow light. The colour of daylight rarely changes as quickly and dramatically as this but it is important to realise that it does change continuously and that colour film will record the changes even when they are quite subtle.

Shooting into the light

Most pictures taken in sunlight have the sun somewhere within an angle of 180° behind the camera. Shooting pictures where the sun is shining towards the camera and behind the subject, is one of the guaranteed ways to get a more dramatic or, at the very least, a more interesting, result. It is by no means a method which can be used all the time and like any other technique it should not be used just for the sake of it but only when it will make a genuine contribution to the picture.

If the sun is to be included in the image, then of course there is no way that the lens can be protected from it and the effects will have to be incorporated into the picture. In practice, you will find that shorter focal length lenses (wide angle) are less prone to flare and more prone to internal reflections than long lenses. On many occasions when the sun is included in the picture its intensity is often reduced by mist, atmospheric haze or its position in the sky. The setting sun is far less threatening than its noonday self. In these situations the effects of flare and internal reflection will be greatly reduced. Another trick is to partially obscure the sun with something in the picture area.

Another problem arising from shooting into the sun is the immense contrast or brightness range of the image. There will be brilliant highlights and dense shadows. It is simply not possible for the film to handle such extremes of brightness. You will have to decide which is the most important, the shadows or the highlights, and calculate the exposure accordingly. If you are taking a portrait, for example, with the sun shining behind the model's head, then the rim of hair will become a bright highlight, but the face itself a shadow area. In this case the exposure required to record the face so the skin tones are a normal density would make the brightly lit hair devoid of detail. If the exposure were calculated to record detail in the hair, then the face would record as a much darker tone. Either could produce a pleasing and effective picture but it is necessary to be aware of the alternatives and to decide which is going to create the result you want.

Having considered some of the problems that can be caused by

Masking the sun with the branches of a tree has avoided excessive flare and retained full contrast in the picture on the left, taken in Copenhagen. Shooting against the light has created a strong textural quality on the cobbled pathway and the dense shadows have given the picture considerable impact. The exposure was calculated for the lighter areas of the subject and a small aperture was chosen to obtain adequate depth of field.

shooting against the light, let us now look at some of the advantages. One good thing about using this method of lighting is that it is often a very effective way of separating the main subject from the background detail, either by creating a rim of light around the subject or by creating light areas in the background against which the subject can be isolated. Backlighting (where the light source is behind the subject) often reduces the range of tones in the subject due to the increase of contrast and this can simplify a complex or fussy image.

A subject which is dependent on a texture can often benefit from backlighting. A low sun skating over wet cobbles towards the camera, for example, can give a dramatic and realistic effect, the strong shadows created becoming a powerful ingredient in the composition.

Using flare

Shooting into the sun presents a few particular problems. Sun shining directly onto the surface of the camera lens causes internal reflections and flare. Internal reflection manifests itself as a series of blobs of light sometimes echoing the shape of the iris. Flare is an overall fogging effect which reduces most of the contrast. Modern methods of lens coating greatly reduce these effects, but if the sun is not actually in the picture they can be completely eliminated by an efficient lens hood or even by shielding the lens with your hand. This is a bit tricky with an eye level, handheld camera, but very effective when the lens hood does not quite offer enough protection. Sometimes it is possible to 'hide' the camera in a natural shadow created by the sun, or if you have a companion, to position them

so that they throw a shadow over the lens while remaining outside the picture area.

Sometimes flare and reflection can actually contribute to a photograph and it is worth considering them in this way first of all before deciding to eliminate them. Flare in particular can be very attractive.

A low winter sun partly veiled by cloud has enabled the photographer to shoot directly into the sun with this picture of Venice, and still retain a full tonal range. Correct exposure for this type of scene is critical if adequate detail is to be retained. In this instance, an average was computed from readings taken from the shadowed foreground and the sky.

A near silhouette has been produced by shooting into the light with this picture of a fish farmer on an Israeli Kibbutz. With this type of image the shape or outline of the subject provides most of the interest.

Colour and mood

Not surprisingly, colour has a great influence on our moods. We are surrounded by colours which, albeit subconsciously, condition our responses. Most of these responses are so deeply ingrained that they will override any other considerations. Red, for example, signifies danger or aggression; its use for stop lights and warning signs is universal and it is the most dominant colour in the spectrum. Its role almost certainly dates back to early man's first experience of fire. Red in a picture will always have first claim on the attention. It can even give the impression of coming out of the picture towards the viewer.

Orange and yellow are colours that signify brightness and happiness. Orange is warm and inviting, as opposed to red which is ablaze with dangerous connotations. It is the fire in the hearth as opposed to the forest fire. Yellow is the colour that most children paint the sun.

Green and blue, on the other hand, are relaxing and reassuring, invariably acting as background colours and rarely dominating. In nature, greens and blues are synonymous with repose and harmony. Green fields, blue skies and seas tend to be bathed in colours that we hardly notice but nevertheless reassure us.

As colours become darker and less saturated with light they tend to convey a more sombre mood. Browns, purples and colours that approach black are inclined to create a gloomy or serious atmosphere.

It is not only the colours themselves that affect the mood of the picture but also their intensity or the degree of saturation. Light pastel colours, for example, will create delicate soft pictures. The romantic nudes of David Hamilton are heavily dependent on this use of colour and he has developed a very effective technique to control this aspect of his images.

Strong saturated colours on the other hand create much more assertive images with more immediate impact. The use of colour in many forms of advertising photography, particularly posters is a good example of how the skilful use of vibrant colours can produce compelling images.

It is interesting to explore the possibilities of pictures which con-tain only a minimal amount of colour, where the result is *almost* monochromatic but not quite. Images like this can possess a feeling of mystery and it can be very rewarding to look for and shoot pictures of subjects that have little or no colour content, or where the lighting conditions or mist or rain has subdued the natural colours. Deliberately falsifying colours to create atmosphere should not be ignored. There are many ways in which this can be done, using filters, using the 'wrong' film for the light source, or specialist films such as infra red, mixing different light sources, even simply varying exposures. All of these tricks and many more can provide an almost endless range of effects for the photographer who is prepared to experiment.

Restful and reassuring green sets the mood for this peaceful picture of the Buttes of Montmartre in Paris. Like blue, green is a colour which symbolizes peace and tranquillity, and in this picture the mood is enhanced by the repetition of the vertical lines of the trees and lamp posts. Any form of repetition in a picture tends to create a feeling of harmony and reassurance.

Bold colours (right) create a feeling of liveliness and vitality. This picture was taken for a holiday brochure and the use of bold bright colours is frequently exploited in poster and advertizing photography because it can create a feeling of excitement. The picture was shot on a long lens, using a fairly wide aperture to subdue unwanted detail in the background which in turn throws the sharply focussed models well into the foreground. Back-lighting has avoided hard shadows on the models which would detract from the crisp detail of the faces and colourful shirts.

Pastel colours created in this picture by a combination of soft focus, soft lighting and overexposure, suggests a feeling of romanticism. While bold saturated colours are used in images to create realism and vitality, the opposite techniques are used when a more gentle mood is required. This picture was taken on a Pentax 6 × 7 camera with an old box camera lens mounted and focussed in a cardboard tube. The backlighting has caused a degree of flare in the uncoated lens which has contributed to the soft colours of the image.

Warm and inviting is the feeling suggested by colours like yellow and orange. This studio picture of a model was lit by bouncing two flashes off an orange background, with only reflectors in front. The resulting colour cast seems appropriate to the mood of the picture which although by no means openly provocative has a certain 'come up and see me sometime' feel about it.

The daylight studio

It is natural enough to think in terms of outdoors for daylight photography, but in fact daylight can also be a very effective source of light indoors. A reasonably large window or a skylight can be the basis of an informal but useful home studio and with a few props the range and style of portraits can be greatly expanded.

Screens and backgrounds
The most immediate problem you will encounter is the increase in contrast. This is a natural result of the light being much more concentrated and directional than it is outdoors. However, this is easily overcome by the addition of a few reflectors, which can be made from large sheets of rigid white card, polystyrene or even white-painted hardboard. These can simply be propped against pieces of furniture or a keen DIY person could make up a stand for them. It is also a good idea to have a movable background which can be positioned at any angle to move the camera position and model at will to create a wider range of lighting effects. It also means that you are not restricted to the background provided by the decoration of the room. Its tone and colour can be changed to suit the mood of the picture. Professional photographic stores sell rolls of cartridge paper in a wide range of colours up to three metres wide for making background screens. Alternatively, make up backgrounds using fabric stretched on a frame, or a large sheet of painted hardboard.

The window which is the source of light is obviously fixed and so it is by moving the model and camera position that you can alter the lighting effect. The quality of light which the window provides is of course dependent partly on the lighting conditions outside and partly on the direction the window faces. A north-facing window, for example, will never have direct sunlight through it, but will tend to receive light of a more constant quality. If the room you wish to use as a studio is not north facing you can always control the quality of light by diffusing it through window screens of translucent fabric or even venetian blinds.

The quality of light will also be affected by the distance of the model from the window. Close to, the lighting will tend to be quite hard, further away it will be correspondingly softer, and of course the brightness will also decrease.

Indoor still-lifes
There is no reason, of course, why the daylight studio should be confined to portraits. Window light can be a very useful and effective means of lighting still-life arrangements. With the camera mounted on a tripod and long exposures there can be enough light even on a dull day. A small, movable bench or table is essential, so that the arrangement can be positioned correctly in relation to the light source. In addition to the white reflectors used for lighting up the shadow areas, small mirrors can also be used just outside of the picture area to introduce additional highlights and to give a stronger effect in the shadow areas. These can be most easily positioned and manoeuvred by supporting them on lumps of modelling clay or plasticine. An effect between that of the white reflector and a mirror can be achieved by using crinkled silver paper taped to a board.

It is equally possible to use both mirrors and silver paper to extend the scope of lighting effects on portraits, although of course larger screens will be necessary. In professional photography, the tendency is towards specialization and subjects

A more directional light was used for this portrait of an ex-miner, positioned close to a large window on the left with a white wall immediately behind him. The result is a picture which displays a reasonably good modelling of the face with a fairly strong textural quality.

A candid picture of a young lad having his mid morning pinta at his classroom desk in the classroom. A reasonably fast film, (TRI X in this case) and a room with good window light lets you take pictures like this without artificial lighting.

The high key quality of this picture of a baby was achieved by the use of soft lighting from a window diffused by a fine net curtain, some distance from the bed on which the baby lay. The baby was dressed in white and placed on a white blanket and the soft shadows that were created were further reduced by a white reflector on the right hand side.

like still-life and portraiture are considered as far apart as you can get, but one of the pleasures of amateur photography is to learn a particular technique in one field and then to discover how it can be applied to different subjects and in different conditions.

Photographing nudes

While the daylight studio can be a very convenient way of shooting conventional portraits it can be even more so for nude and glamour photography. Although daylight is an ideal light source for lighting the human body, outdoor locations can have serious drawbacks. The most obvious is simply that on many occasions the weather and the temperature are just not pleasant enough to allow the model to relax and look comfortable. Secondly, lack of facilities for renewing make-up, changing clothes and adjusting hair can be difficult on location. Above all, however, it is the plain fact that an outdoor location is often just inappropriate to the theme or mood of a picture and the greater degree of control over backgrounds and props that can be found in the daylight studio makes it particularly suitable for nude photography. The only additional requirement is rather more space than would be needed for a head and shoulder portrait and of course correspondingly larger reflectors and backgrounds.

A white reflector was used to throw back some light into the shadows of this shot of a girl sitting in a recessed window. Without the reflector, the shot would be a near silhouette, as the camera is aimed almost directly into the light source. Exposure measurement needs to be made quite carefully in these cases as the brilliant light coming from behind the model could induce underexposure. The safest method is to take a close-up reading from the subjects skin, ensuring that the direct light from the window does not reach the meter.

An open doorway provided both the lighting and the setting for this still-life trouvé, found in a small Spanish village. In many ways this type of still-life subject is better shot with natural light. Somehow things like flowers and fruit look best lit with daylight, and professional still-life photographers often go to a great deal of trouble and expense to simulate the quality of daylight in their studios. The only real disadvantage with daylight is that it does not have a constant colour and intensity and is less controllable but it offers a very satisfactory alternative to studio lighting equipment.

Colour and detail

One of the problems that shooting in colour brings for the photographer who wants to create interesting and exciting pictures, is that it is too literal. Colour film records and reproduces fairly accurately the colours of the world around us, often making it too real to allow personal expression and interpretation to blossom. For creative photography, something must be left to the viewer's imagination and sometimes the stark reality of the colour process is a barrier to this. Many leading photographers choose to do their more expressive work in black and white for this reason.

One of the many ways to overcome this drawback when working in colour is to deliberately look for pictures which isolate small elements of a subject and to present them in such a way that their original role or importance is changed. By doing so, the resulting picture can take on a new meaning, and present a personal statement.

All that is really involved is to learn to look not only at the subject itself but also at its components, to see how they can become the subject, and how by isolating and emphasizing them, a completely new response can be evoked. It's a sad fact that familiarity does indeed breed contempt. Many everyday surroundings go largely unnoticed and often it is only by going to a new environment that people can be stimulated into taking a fresh look at things. But remember that one man's familiar is another's stimulation and looking for the sort of pictures on these pages could result in the discovery of a wealth of new subject matter right on your own doorstep.

For the novice, the awareness and experience of colour and composition that can be gained by producing this type of image is invaluable.

Numbers and letters always attract attention and when used as part of a composition as in this picture the effect can be quite striking. Again, this type of image needs to be in sharp focus and in this case a special film produced by Kodak for photomicrography was used. It is very sharp and very fine grained, more so than Kodachrome, and has a speed of 16 ASA. It has a magenta colour cast which can be corrected by a greenish filter.

Condensation on a window has been used as a diffusion screen for this view of a sunlit tree in the garden. This effect has reduced the image to a vague suggestion of light and shape with only the droplets on the window being in sharp focus. A fairly wide aperture was chosen to show up the condensation in relief against the background.

A venetian blind makes a very effective image. The strong contrast between the red blind and the blue wall is an important element and the position of the broken slat makes an effective centre of interest because it breaks into the otherwise ordered lines in the picture. This picture was also shot on the Kodak photomicrographic film, which has helped to produce the strongly contrasting, heavily saturated colour quality.

A peeling poster has resulted in an almost abstract image. The use of only one colour with white and black shapes creates a quite dramatic effect. A photograph like this needs to be really crisp and sharp and a fine grained film like Kodachrome will often give the best result.

Rusty railings leaning against a wall, their shadow causing an almost double image effect, has created a quite delicate, sketch-like image. The limited colour range enhances this effect even further. This picture was found in the corner of a builder's yard, not the type of location that springs immediately to mind as a photographers venue but as the saying goes 'beauty is in the eye of the beholder

THE ART OF COMPOSITION

Composition is simply the technique of arranging the ingredients of an image in the most effective and pleasing way. It involves first of all becoming aware of these ingredients, deciding their relative importance and then creating a sense of order and harmony with them. This may sound rather complex, but most people are subconsciously composing things every day, putting fruit into a bowl, flowers into a vase, laying out a business letter, planting a flower border. These are all examples of composition. The composition of a photograph is simply a matter of applying the same sort of thought and care.

Simplicity is the keynote of this picture and it follows quite closely the golden rules. The lone tree is positioned at the intersection of thirds, and the main lines of the picture also intersect the edges of the frame at this same point.

A much busier picture has resulted in this shot of almond blossom trees. The main tree is still at the intersection of thirds, its white blossom is strongly contrasted against the darker tones of the mountain behind.

Basic principles

The 'golden rule' of composition is that the main point of interest should be at the intersection of thirds. This simply means that the main subject should stand at the intersection of imaginary lines drawn vertically and horizontally a third of a way along the sides of the picture. It is easy to dismiss this as dogmatic nonsense, but if you look through a large number of good photographs a high proportion of them will conform to this rule. It is of course equally true that there are very many fine pictures which completely reject this formula. The answer is really that ultimately you must allow your own taste and judgement to decide the issue, otherwise you will not have the opportunity to develop your own ideas and style.

Another of the rules is that the eye should be led towards the centre of interest and distracting elements such as bright highlights or dominant shapes and colours should be kept away from the edges of the picture. There are several ways in which the eye can be attracted to the main subject. You could use perspective lines to lead towards it. Another method is to contrast the main interest in some way with the rest of the picture. This can be done tonally, for example a light subject against a predominately dark background will draw the eye towards it. Even shapes can provide contrast. An orange surrounded by children's building blocks will automatically attract the viewer's attention by its roundness in a square world.

Colour is probably one of the strongest influences in attracting the eye and if the main point of interest is of a contrasting colour to the rest of the picture, this can easily override any other influences. When shooting in colour the arrangement and distribution of colours within the image should be the first thing to consider in terms of composition.

A different image, but the same formula still applies to this picture of two people taking a stroll in an Alpine meadow. They contrast against the background, they are positioned at the intersection of thirds, and the shaft of sunlight skimming down the mountainside leads the eye directly towards them.

Colour and contrast

There are three basic ways in which colours react with each other. They either clash discordantly, or they harmonize, or they contrast with each other. Colours which clash are generally to be avoided in photography as they will simply fight against each other and create a feeling of disorder in the picture. However, even this quality can be exploited and used to create very effective images by a perceptive photographer. The majority of good colour photographs, however, owe their success to contrast or harmony.

Contrast is created between colours when the two hues are complementary to each other. Imagine that the colours of the spectrum are made into a circle so that red is at, say, 12 o'clock and the colours progress round through the changes of orange, yellow, blue, indigo until violet finishes up at 11 o'clock. The complementary colours will then be found opposite each other. Opposite red will be a greenish blue called cyan, opposite green will be a reddish blue called magenta and opposite blue is yellow. The strongest contrast will exist where the colours are diametrically opposed, but a degree of contrast will exist several shades either side of the opposite. The strongest contrast is also only possible when both of the colours are fully saturated.

You must also consider the relative dominance of the contrasting colours. The 'warm' colours of the spectrum, yellow, orange, red etc. are more dominant than the 'cool' colours such as blue and green, and this is a vital consideration when composing a picture in colour. For example, a yacht with a bright red sail tacking on a cyan sea will be more assertive because red is much more dominant than cyan. If the situation were reversed and a girl wearing a cyan dress were photographed standing against a red background the eye would be far less strongly attracted to the main point of interest.

Natural contrast is often provided by nature as in this Norfolk landscape of red poppies against green grass and blue sea and sky. Although this combination of colours represents an extreme in terms of contrast, the overall effect is not garish as the red flowers are scattered and their colour impact is softened by the surrounding grass. A polarizing filter was used to strengthen the colour of the sea and sky. This kind of filter can often be very useful with pictures where there is a lot of reflected light, such as sea and mountain scenes.

The warm coloured stone of this Parisian building does not provide a true contrast to the red blind, but the small patch of red still has a powerful claim on our attention. Its importance is underlined by its position in the frame, at the inter-section of thirds, which is considered to be the point at which the main subject should be in a balanced composition. A long lens was used in this picture to isolate a relatively small area of the building.

The attraction of red is the strongest of all the colours, particularly when set against a contrasting background as in this picture taken in Crete, where the Aegean sea provides an almost primary blue background to the tiny red pedalo. In this picture the red *is* the main point of interest but if it were an unintentional detail in the background it would be a serious distraction. It should be remembered that red always attracts the eye and if there is red in your picture it should always be on or near the main subject.

The many coloured coats of these skiers waiting for the lift could easily have produced a jumbled and confusing image, but the plain white background provided by the snow has enabled the contrasting colours and the shapes they make to be separated and defined clearly, resulting in an orderly picture. When calculating exposures in this type of situation it is important not to be misled by the brilliance of the snow. A straightforward reading will result in underexposure and bright colours like these need to be given adequate exposure. It is best to take a close-up reading first and then move back to the position from which you want to shoot.

Composing a still-life

In most areas of photography there is a limited degree of control over the elements of the picture. Still-life photography offers the opportunity to control every aspect of the image, and so it is an excellent means of gaining experience and developing the technique of composition as well as an understanding of light.

The first essential is a firm support for the subject, such as a table or bench of a convenient height. Next comes the light source. The photographer's control begins with the choice of the objects to be photographed, and the background and surface against which they are to be displayed. The inexperienced photographer should begin with say three or four simple objects of varying size and shape, and a relatively plain background, possibly fabric, paper or wood. The camera must be supported on a tripod, as the photographer will have to move backwards and forwards between the still-life bench and the camera to make adjustments and view the resulting composition.

Once the background is in position on the table, the next step is to place the largest or most dominant object on it. View this through the camera, and then take one of the other objects and position it in relation to the first. When you are happy with the juxtaposition of the first two objects you may begin to add the others. More than likely you will find that you will want at some stage to reposition one or both of the first elements. This does not matter at all. You have established a starting point and are now beginning to see all of the elements in their total context, and this is really what composition is all about. It will soon become apparent that it is not only the shapes of the objects that decide their positions but their form, their texture and even the shadows which they create. The joy of still-life photography is that you can play around for hours with a small group of simple elements, discarding, changing, adding extra things, altering the backgrounds and finish up, maybe, not even having taken a picture, but having learned a great deal about composition.

One at a time: that was how each item was added to produce the picture at the top. To introduce a little more impact, a tighter crop was tried, resulting in the picture above left. The shot above right was an attempt to add interest. The final picture on the right was created by shooting from a much lower viewpoint.

Colour harmony

Colours harmonize with each other when they come from the same segments of the spectrum circle. For example a picture of red apples, oranges and yellow bananas will have colours in harmony, but if the apples were green there would be an element of contrast. This is equally true wherever the segment is taken in the circle. It is possible for harmony to exist even when the segment is so large that it begins to include contrasting colours, providing the transition and distribution of the colours is complementary to the composition.

The effect of colour contrast is almost totally dependent on the colours themselves and beyond isolating and selecting them the photographer has little control. However, there are a number of factors that can introduce colour harmony into a picture even when it doesn't exist naturally. Fully saturated colours are much less likely to harmonize than colours which are muted, so that any technique which reduces colour saturation can be helpful in creating harmony. Simply overexposing is one method which can be employed under some circumstances. Obviously this is not always appropriate and in subjects with important highlight areas or a wide contrast range it would not be possible.

Soft focus or diffusion is a technique which can be very effective in helping to create harmony even when strong colours are present. You can do this by using a soft focus attachment, or even scotch tape or vaseline in front of the lens. A similar diffusing effect can sometimes be achieved by shooting through an out of focus foreground.

Subject movement is also something which can help to blend unharmonious colours together as the blurring of a moving foreground subject, a boy on a swing for example will create a mix of colours against the background. An overall colour cast created by lighting or filtration will also tend to impose harmony on the colours in a subject. The warmth of evening sunlight is a good example. Or you can shoot daylight film in tungsten light, and vice-versa, and achieve effective results. These are fairly strong measures and often the discreet use of a correction filter may be all that is necessary to create some harmony in a photograph.

The technique of using flare described on page 57 is particularly effective in softening strong colours and helping to blend them. Making use of the weather by shooting in rain, mist or fog is another method of introducing harmony.

Mist and fog can create harmony in a picture because it weakens the colours and creates a softer image. In this autumn landscape, the mist has reduced the colour of the dead leaves to a pale orange and the black trunks of the trees to a greenish grey. Without the mist, the picture would have been quite brightly saturated but its presence has produced an image which is almost monochromatic. Exposure for a scene like this is quite critical, too much and the photograph becomes pale and wishy-washy, too little and it becomes muddy and murky. A safe method is to take an average reading from the brightest and darkest areas.

A colour cast can also impose a quality of harmony on a scene. This picture taken for a holiday brochure on a beach in Majorca has a strong orange colour bias as a result of the colour content of the setting sun. All the colours in the picture have in effect an overall orange tint laid over them causing them all to blend together.
Earlier in the day when the sunlight was of 'standard' colour quality the same scene would have had quite boldly contrasting colours, blue sea and sky, yellow sand and the skin tones and clothes of the models. In fact, a quite different picture would have resulted.

Soft focus is a technique which can be used to help blend the colours of a subject harmoniously. This picture was taken with Scotch tape stretched across the front of the lens diffusing the image, making the colours slightly softer or desaturated, and causing the highlights and lighter colours of the image to 'bleed' slightly into the darker tones. A long focal length lens and a fairly wide aperture was used for this picture, throwing the background detail completely out of focus. The scotch tape technique is also more effective when used with longer lenses and wide apertures.

Careful selection of the subject matter has resulted in this picture having an harmonious quality. If the camera had been aimed slightly further to the right, a bright red hut would have been included which would have completely destroyed the effect of this photograph. A long lens was used to enable a small area of the scene to be isolated. The ability to choose which parts of the subject are to be included in the picture and how it should be framed is always the photographer's greatest area of control and his most important decision.

Viewpoint and composition

In most types of photography, other than still-life and portraiture, the photographer has a relatively limited degree of control over the elements of the image and their composition. With a landscape subject, for example, the only thing that can be changed at will is the position of the camera. The viewpoint therefore becomes the most important decision the photographer can make. Even the lighting can be controlled to a certain degree by the choice of viewpoint.

Most pictures consist of a foreground area or object, middle distance detail and a background.

If, for example, you have an image which comprises of a river in the foreground, a bridge in the middle distance and a church in the background, your choice of viewpoint can yield a surprising number of alternative arrangements. If you were to stand close to the river you would have only water in the foreground. If you stood back a little you may be able to include a fence or some flowers on the bank. By positioning the camera very low you would be able to eliminate the water altogether and with a high camera position the area of water would be increased. By walking along the river bank in one direction you will have the bridge on the right hand side of the picture and from the other direction the bridge would be on the left hand side. From a position close to the bridge the church may be almost behind it and from further along the bank the church would be on one side of the picture and the bridge on the other.

It can be quite tempting, when confronted with an interesting subject simply to raise the camera and shoot it, but it is only by exploring all the possibilities that the choice of viewpoint offers that you will begin to get the very best pictures.

A slight change of viewpoint has resulted in the quite dramatic change in the composition of these two pictures of Linderhof Castle in Bavaria. The second picture involved moving only a dozen paces to the left which brought the statue into the foreground, not only creating a more dramatic picture but giving a greater feeling of depth. A small aperture was chosen to obtain enough depth of field to render both the foreground statue and the distant building sharp. Never simply accept the first and perhaps most obvious viewpoint for a shot, but always look for alternatives. It usually takes only a minute or two and will often yield a better picture.

A total change of viewpoint in these two pictures of a pigeon fancier in a Paris park was required in this case. The first picture (left), although promising, was felt to have a rather cluttered and obtrusive background which detracted from the subject itself. Even with a long lens and a wide aperture there still seemed to be too much going on in the background. Fortunately, the man was so preoccupied with his friends that there was time for the photographer to move right around his subject and shoot the picture from a completely opposite direction, providing a much less cluttered background and a more clearly defined and interesting shape to the picture. Because the man was then not facing towards the camera it was possible to approach more closely without disturbing him, resulting in a rather more intimate picture.

Composition for dramatic effect

While following the basic rules of composition will usually produce a pleasing and safe result, it is sometimes by going against them that the really dramatic and exciting pictures can be produced. Simply by moving the main subject from the intersection of thirds to, say, the centre on the top right corner of the picture can suggest a completely different way of looking at the image. It is really by introducing an element of surprise rather than following the predictable arrangement of the classic compositions that you can begin to produce pictures that will have an immediate impact. In landscape photography, for example, the horizon is almost always placed either above or below the centre of the frame. If you place the horizon along the centre the viewer will immediately react because it is unexpected. Of course this alone is not enough, the rest of the picture must still balance and

harmonize. To a certain extent the rules of composition are decreed by current fashions and it is only because some people have been prepared to go against them that things change and progress.

It is the photographer who is continually aware of the possibilities and is willing to explore them all and to experiment who is most likely to develop a style of his own and produce exciting and original photographs. Professional photographers are often prepared (and able to afford) to shoot many rolls of film on the same subject. This is not to ensure that 'one comes out' but to be certain that every possible line of approach has been exploited and through this the best possible result obtained. The amateur photographer does not necessarily have to shoot all the alternatives, but he should explore them all even if he saves his film for what he feels is the best picture.

Half and half is not normally a recommended division of interest in a picture, as there is a tendency for both halves to fight for attention and neither to win. This picture works, however, because the main interest is so boldly contrasted in colour, tone, and shape against the rest of the image, and the feeling of space created by the large area of sky and the white arches makes the presence of the people even stronger. This picture was shot on a wide angle lens and the camera tilted upwards to include a large area of sky. The blue cast caused by light reflected from the sky into the shaded areas has given further emphasis to the tanned body and red dress.

A strong diagonal line is always a powerful element in the composition of a picture, creating a vigorous and dramatic effect. This photograph of the street of the Knights of St John in Rhodes was shot on a wide angle lens to exaggerate the effect of perspective and also the effect of the diagonal. The great depth of field obtained with such a lens also enables the strongly textured detail of the backlit cobbled surface to be recorded sharply from close-up foreground to the far distance.

Contrasting shapes have been used in this picture taken in a builder's yard. It is composed mainly of rectangular shapes and the inclusion of the curved roof of the distant building immediately attracts the attention. This building contrasts in colour as well as shape with the red and yellow bricks. It is this combination of contrasting qualities that is the most powerful element in composition.

Framing the picture

A very effective and useful device in the technique of composition is to use something in the foreground to create a frame around the image. It helps to prevent the eye from straying away from the main interest and can generate a feeling of harmony within the image. The framing device does not have to completely surround the picture. It may extend only along the sides or along the top of the picture. Apart from its usefulness as an aid to composition, it can be an effective means of creating a feeling of depth in the picture. It is important that this frame should be a complement to the subject and not a distraction and that its shape and tone should be in harmony with it. Often only a silhouette may be necessary, a picture for example of a view shot through the archway of a door or a window can add a great deal to the interest of a photograph. It is a particularly useful technique in landscape and architectural photography. It is usually possible to find something like an overhanging branch or a beam which can help to contain the picture and relieve the boredom of a blank sky.

A frame can also be used along the sides and base of a picture. In portraiture, for example, it is possible to use the model's arm and shoulder in such a way, and in very close-up shots the model's hair can act as a frame. With studio lighting it is possible to produce a frame tonally, by creating a lighter tone immediately behind the model and allowing it to become much darker along the sides and top of the picture. Portrait photographers often use a small spot light hidden behind the model and directed at the background to achieve this effect.

The dominant frame to this picture of the Israel Knesset in Jerusalem (above left) is provided by the gateway of the complex. The fact that the frame has almost taken over the picture is justified by the intended relationship between the shapes in the architect's concept.

A frame within the image has been used to create a quite ordered composition of the ruined city of Avdat in the Negev desert (far left). In this case the framing device, the archway, has been allowed to retain some detail and texture.

Through a window or doorway is perhaps the most basic and obvious method of creating a frame but the lettering on the glass has given this picture (left) a rather unusual slant.

The framing effect can be quite clearly seen in these two Austrian landscapes. The picture above is quite pleasing but by a shift of viewpoint to the right, the photographer has been able to include a frame in the second picture (right).

The centrally placed subject is not generally recommended by the rule makers, but it can sometimes work. This picture is almost totally symmetrical which could easily be boring, but the element of contrast provided by the round face and red jumper of the old lady is enhanced by the surrounding rectangular shapes of the blue-grey frontage of her home.

A low viewpoint almost always introduces an element of drama into a picture and this picture of kids in London's East End was shot from pavement level using a wide angle lens. It was a staged picture as it involved the co-operation of the children who were asked to play 'jumping the cracks' for a book illustration, but after a few minutes they became absorbed in the game.

Tucked into the corner is another position for the subject which is considered undesirable by the orthodox, particularly when there is a distracting element in the centre of the picture, like the candles in this picture of the Guardian of a Tomb in Israel. There is an element of conflict in this picture which appealed to the photographer. It would have been quite easy to have moved to one side and excluded the candles, cropped more tightly and avoided the vast area of wall and there would be a pleasant picture of an interesting old man; but this composition makes it a little more intriguing.

A teasing picture like this shot of a young village girl in Morocco makes you almost look twice to be sure you've seen it. It could easily be a disaster for the subject of your picture to occupy only about one percent of the picture area but the single, dark eye of the shy but curious girl still manages to stand out from the colourful doorway in which she is hiding. Luck and anticipation are two invaluable commodities in photography and this picture is a good example of both.

Choosing the moment

Unlike the other arts, photography is concerned less with imagination than with observation. It is a means of producing an image from the things around us and is therefore dependent on the existence of real objects. But even though a photograph simply records an image of something which exists, it is very important to be aware that things exist not only in space but also in time. To many photographers, it is the ability of the photographic process to isolate and record an image at a precise and often unique moment in time that constitutes its greatest quality, in creative terms. A mountain may exist for a million years, but the way it appears from a particular place, in a particular light, at a given moment in time, is completely unique; it will never look that way again. It is the ability of the camera to capture these never to be repeated events that has been its strongest appeal to the majority of the great photographers.

You must try to be simultaneously aware not only of the elements of the image, of the composition and the light, but also how their relationship is affected by the passage of time. Often when shooting pictures there is a sense of 'coming together'. Things over which one has little or no control can sometimes almost be willed into doing what is needed. There is always an optimum moment when everything has combined to the greatest effect, and after which they recede. Professional photographers, whose livelihood depends upon getting good results every time, often shoot reels and reels of film, because during the build-up period the results will become progressively better and if *the* moment never happens they

will at least have something. Even when confronted with a dozen strips of film of a fairly simple subject, a fashion shot against a plain background for example, it is surprising how easily the best frame can be found. It may just be the turn of a head, a fleeting expression or the swirl of a skirt, but something at a particular moment will single out that one image from all of the others. This does not mean that the keen amateur must shoot reels and reels on each subject, but you should always be aware of the effect of time and be ready for that one perfect moment.

It was the great French photographer Henri Cartier-Bresson who coined the phrase 'the decisive moment' and it is indeed this moment of decision which, in most cases, determines a great picture. No other medium in the visual arts has this capability and it is the exploitation of this quality which fully realizes the potential of photography.

Anticipating the moment was necessary with these two pictures of the old lady and the children photographed in Naples. The photographer felt there was a picture with both the old lady and the children together, but the children kept hogging the camera, much to the old lady's annoyance. During this period the photographer made several exposures, of which the smaller picture is one, which were quite pleasing but he knew it could be better. Quite suddenly the children spontaneously and without being asked grouped themselves each side of the old lady, making a frame and also placing all the heads in a row. It lasted for only a second and afterwards the children were all over the place again, but it was there for long enough to make an exposure and to take a good picture.

A question of balance decided when this picture of Hastings Pier was taken. The light was good and the pier was creating a strong composition in the view-finder but something else was needed, something which would balance the picture. Unexpectedly and inexplicably a lone cyclist appeared, pedalling along the firm sand towards the pier. All the photographer had to do was to wait until the cyclist appeared in the viewfinder, and at the moment he reached the point of balance, make the exposure. One second before, or after, that moment and the effect of this picture would have been completely changed.

Uncontrollable elements are often the factors upon which a successful picture depends and luck can play as important a role in picture making as any photographic skills. It is, however, necessary to recognize these happenings and to be ready to take advantage. The picture of the old lady and the cat taken, in the Mea Sherim in Jerusalem, is dependent on their juxtaposition, back to back, both bending over their supper. It was the moment that this happened that the picture was created, something over which the photographer had no control, but never-theless was ready to shoot when it happened.

THE CREATIVE CAMERA

Camera controls are provided to enable you to consistently produce correctly exposed and sharply defined images. However, these same controls—shutter speed, aperture and focussing can also be used to create a wide range of effects.

A slow shutter speed, and a panning camera has resulted in the sharp image of the car set against a very blurred background. Using this technique creates an impression of movement which enhances the quality of the photograph. In this instance a shutter speed 1/15th second was used.

A moving subject, a stationary camera, and a slow shutter speed have combined to create this evocative image of wheat waving in a summer breeze. The camera was mounted on a tripod and an exposure of about 1/4 second was given. Part of the effect of this picture is due to the fact that although the ears of the wheat are moving quite vigorously, the stems are almost still at their base, which creates various degrees of blur within the same image. A series of pictures were taken at the same time with slight variations in the shutter speed.

An almost abstract image has resulted in this picture of hockey players. A slow shutter speed of 1/8 second was used with a panned camera. Results under these conditions are often rather unpredictable. However, they can convey a dramatic impression of movement.

Shutter speed and movement

The choice of a shutter speed is a lot more important than merely insuring the right exposure. One of the unique qualities of the photographic process is its ability to record movement. Indeed, many things were not possible to see, let alone record, until the invention of photography. It is now commonplace for photography to be used to determine the winner in a close-finish horse race for example, and anyone with even a modest camera can capture and record moments of movement and action that cannot be seen with the naked eye.

How movement is recorded is directly dependent on the choice of shutter speed. The first and perhaps most obvious choice is to use the fastest possible speed on the camera to freeze the action completely. Most modern cameras beyond the very simplest can provide an exposure as brief as 1/500 second and many 1/1000 or 1/2000. In most circumstances, the majority of normal movements can be stopped at these speeds. If the intention is to freeze a moment of action, then the safest way is to set the fastest shutter speed, follow the movement by panning the camera (with the subject) and waiting until the movement is at its peak or its slowest before exposing. Even a galloping horse can be recorded more sharply if it is photographed when all four hoofs are on the ground rather than when the legs are moving. There is always a point at which a moving object can be recorded more sharply, even when a relatively slow shutter speed is used, for example a racing car when it is cornering, a sprinter between strides, a child on a swing just before it descends. All that is necessary is to anticipate correctly

and to release the shutter at precisely the right moment.

It is not always possible to pan the camera with a moving subject and on these occasions you must anticipate the spot where the picture is to be taken, sight and prefocus the camera and wait until the subject appears in the viewfinder. When the subject is moving and the camera is stationary a higher shutter speed is needed to freeze the action. The necessary exposure will not only be dependent on the speed of the moving object but also its direction. Someone running towards the camera could be sharply recorded at say 1/125 second, but if he were running at the same speed directly across the camera's view, a speed of 1/500 second could be necessary

However, a completely sharp image of a moving object is not always the best method of expressing speed and movement in a photograph. Such an image of even a very quickly moving subject can often appear to be stationary. A much more dramatic and evocative effect can be achieved by using a slower shutter speed and allowing a controlled degree of blur to affect the image. This is usually done by choosing a shutter speed which is fast enough to record the more static elements of a moving subject sharply, for example the head and torso of a running man, but slow enough to allow a degree of blur to affect the limbs. By panning the camera at the same speed as the runner the background will also become blurred. It is not possible to give sensible indications of what speeds are necessary to achieve optimum results as there are so many variable factors and you must try to reach a compromise between a basic sharpness in the main areas of the subject and a pleasing degree of blur in the perimeters and background. With a subject that is moving in one plane only such as a racing car travelling across the camera's view, it is quite possible to get an acceptably sharp picture of the whole car (apart from the wheels of course) at shutter speeds of 1/30 and 1/15 second if the panning is carried out effectively. With a subject such as a running horse where the legs are travelling in a different plane to the body all sorts of often unpredictable blurring will occur at the slower shutter speeds even with the panning technique, but this can be extremely effective, if not totally controllable.

Depth of field

As with the shutter speed, the aperture offers a very important facility to the photographer in addition to the control of exposure. The degree of sharpness that extends before and beyond the point of focus is directly dependent on the size of the aperture. With a very wide aperture, say f.2, the plane of sharp focus will be very shallow but the range of sharpness will increase progressively as the size of the aperture is reduced. This plane of optimum definition is called depth of field and it is also dependent on two other factors. The further away the point of focus is from the camera the greater becomes the depth of field. This can be seen readily on a camera with a focussing screen such as a single lens reflex. If you were to focus on the eyes of a model close up to the camera at full aperture the tip of the nose and the ears would be distinctly unsharp, but at a distance of say six metres, not only the model but objects immediately in front and behind will be completely sharp.

The other consideration when dealing with depth of field is that it is not evenly distributed either side of the point of focus but is greater behind than in front, approximately one third in front and two thirds behind. It can be seen from this that if you wish to record an image with the maximum degree of depth of field you should use the smallest possible aperture and focus on a point at about a third of the distance between the camera and the furthest object. Cameras that have a focussing facility but not a screen, usually have a depth of field scale engraved on the focussing mount and you can read off the range of sharp focus against the aperture in use.

Depth of field can obviously be used not only for achieving a maximum range of sharpness but also to get the greatest effect from a shallow plane of focus. By focussing at relatively close distances and using a wide aperture, backgrounds can be reduced to just a vague blur. This is a particularly useful technique in outdoor portraits where a fussy detailed background can seriously detract from the importance of the face. But of course this technique can be applied equally effectively to any subject where it is desirable to isolate and emphasize the main point of interest from its surroundings.

Minimum and maximum depth of field are illustrated in these two pictures. The shot on the left was made using the smallest aperture on the lens (f.22) and the shot on the right was wide open (f.3.5).

Maximum depth of field was needed for this close-up shot of ivy leaves although there was only a matter of a few centimetres between the foreground and background. The depth of field decreases dramatically when the lens is focussed at closer distances and although the lens was stopped down to f.16, the furthest leaves in the background are still not sharp.

Maximum depth of field was used to obtain adequate definition in both foreground and distant detail in this picture of London's Big Ben. A wide angle lens was used at its smallest aperture of f.16 and was focussed at about one metre. The foregound was about 50 cm away.

Creative exposure

In purely technical terms it is true to say that there is such a thing as a 'correct' exposure under a given set of circumstances. It would be the exposure that most effectively and accurately reproduces the range of tones and colours to the best of the film's ability. Where a technically accurate reproduction is necessary, a photograph of a painting for example, it can only be done by working under very tightly controlled conditions, with carefully balanced lighting, film which has been previously tested for speed and colour balance and precisely regulated processing conditions. Only then is it possible to say with any confidence that you have made a correct exposure. Most photographs taken by most photographers are simply not like that, and the controlled conditions that are necessary to ensure accurate reproduction are not possible for normal situations. Even if they were, an accurate reproduction is not what is usually required. Most photographers simply want a result which pleases them, one which reflects their impression of what they saw, not just a carbon copy of it. Under these circumstances the correct exposure is the one that achieves this result, although in technical terms it may well be 'wrong'. It is a mistake to become over concerned with technical accuracy, or you can become like the hi-fi fanatics who are so busy listening for wow and flutter that they just don't hear the music.

The best way to develop an exposure technique which constantly gives you the quality you want and the results you have visualized, is to first find a film you like. They all have slightly different characteristics. Some you may find pleasing and others not. The next thing is to become familiar with it. Use it under as many different conditions

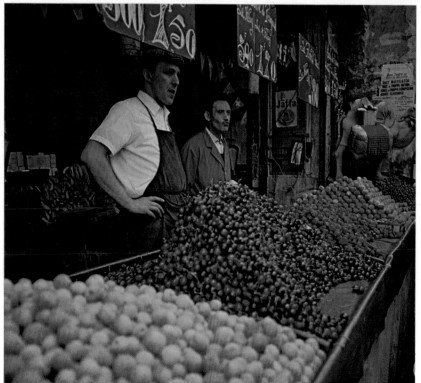

Right and wrong exposure would be difficult to attribute to the two pictures above of the woodland scene, although there is 1 stop difference in the two exposures. Each exposure has its merits.

Deliberate underexposure has been employed to create richly saturated colours in the photograph of the French street market scene (left). The relatively soft lighting has produced a low contrast range, where underexposure has prevented the shadows from completely blocking up.

Deliberate overexposure of the photograph of the girl (above right) has created an almost romantic image with soft pastel colours and delicate tones. Shooting into the light and allowing a certain amount of flare to occur has kept the contrast level of the image quite low.

Dramatic underexposure of the seascape has converted what was in fact a bright sunlit beach in Cornwall to an almost threatening stormy picture. In this instance shooting into the light has created such bright highlights on the water that they have remained so, in spite of being underexposed.

as you can, find out what happens when you overexpose it or under-expose it, whether it gives a good neutral tone on a grey day or goes green or magenta. Whatever happens it is vital that you know so that in the future you can use its characteristics to work for you. It may be that you will find one type of film better for portraits and another for landscapes and even a third or fourth for night shots or close-ups. It is not until you become familiar with the film you use that you can begin to predict the quality of your results, to know that half a stop more exposure will give soft pastel colours and not just washed out hues, or that half a stop less will produce rich tones and not murky blue shadows. Although it may seem wasteful it is best always where possible even with familiar films, to bracket exposures, giving say half a stop more and half a stop less as well as the one you have calculated.

The same make of film can vary 1/3 stop or more from batch to batch and it is equally possible for processing laboratories to produce similar variations. The age and freshness of the film will also affect its speed and colour balance. Try to buy your films as fresh as possible from a reliable dealer, and it is well worth your while to buy as many as you can afford of the same batch and keep them refrigerated until they are needed.

Point of focus

A major difference between the human eyes and a camera is that the eyes seem to see everything from near objects to distant sharply. This is achieved by a spontaneous and imperceptible change in focus which is mostly entirely subconscious. The camera lens cannot do this. It has to be focussed on a specific point at a determined distance from the camera. Anything nearer or further than this will be less sharp. Close to the point of focus the deterioration in sharpness will be barely noticeable, but objects much further or nearer will become distinctly blurred.

Choosing where the camera should be sharply focussed is a vital control in the making of an image. It is a basic technique which enables the photographer to give emphasis to one part of the subject and to subdue others. In many pictures, distant scenes for example, the tendency is to just get everything sharp, but there are many occasions when the inclusion of an unsharp foreground would help to emphasize the distant view. When taking a portrait out of doors the same principle can be applied in reverse by ensuring that the background is far enough behind the model to become unsharp, thus emphasising the focussed face.

In these examples the unsharp elements of a picture play a negative role, but lack of definition in an image can be a very positive factor in producing a successful photograph. A picture which is sharp overall more closely resembles the scene we saw, it is in fact closer to reality, especially in a colour photograph. This 'realistic' quality can often be a barrier to the photographer who wants to produce images that do more than simply record a scene. The discreet and sensitive use of areas of unsharpness in a picture can be a crucial factor in creating mood and producing images that leave something to the viewer's imagination.

Foreground sharp with a blurred background and vice-versa. These two pictures, taken in a playing field, demonstrate the importance of where to focus. The two images each have a quite different quality which results solely from the focussing of the lens. These pictures were taken with an SLR where it is easy to see the focussing effect on the camera's viewing screen. With a viewfinder camera, however, it is . . . . . . necessary to be aware that this effect occurs and to visualize the result before you shoot, as this type of viewfinder can give the beginner the impression that everything will be equally sharp.

Where to focus was the decision the photographer had to make pretty swiftly in this shot of two Orthodox Jews taken in Jerusalem. Focussing on the furthest face has automatically made this the main subject of the picture; the other man's face simply becomes a compositional foil. A fairly long lens was used for this shot and this, combined with a wide aperture, has sharpened the effect of the focussed part of the picture—the lines and texture of the face.

Now you see it now you don't, these two pictures of a tennis court fence are another demonstration of how dramatically the point of focus can affect the nature of a photograph. This is an extreme example, but it produces a creative picture.

Filters for colour

The use of filters with colour film is somewhat more limited than it is in black and white photographs, because any colour filter which is introduced will affect the whole image and simply produce an overall colour cast. It is not possible for an ordinary coloured filter to affect the image selectively.

The most useful application of colour filters with colour film is to correct the balance between the light source and the film. Daylight colour film is designed to give optimum results with noon sunlight and when conditions differ from this the film will show a colour cast. This can be corrected by using colour correction filters. They can be bought in the more commonly used colours as mounted glass discs but also in a very wide range of colours and densities in thin gelatine squares which can be slotted into a special mount and fitted onto the camera lens.

When correcting a colour cast, use a filter of the opposite or complementary colour. The blue cast which can result from an overcast sky for example can be corrected with a pale yellowish filter and conversely the yellow cast of evening sunlight can be corrected with a bluish coloured filter. Sometimes it is the colour cast created by the light source which makes a scene attractive and often it can be improved by giving it a little help with a filter. The slight blue cast of a landscape at dusk for example can sometimes simply look a bit flat and grey on film and the discreet use of a light blue filter can often improve things considerably. Similarly, a sunset may be a little less rosy and dramatic than your fond memories when you see the developed film, and the judicious use of a red filter can create that extra touch of drama.

One widely used correction filter is the ultra violet which is designed to reduce the invisible UV light content of daylight which can affect colour film adversely, producing a slight blue cast. It is particularly evident at high altitudes. The advantage of this filter is that it has no noticeable effect in situations where it is not needed and many photographers leave them permanently in position. They also offer some protection to expsnsive lenses.

The other useful application of correction filters is to convert a film for use with a light source other than for which it was designed. For example, if your camera is loaded with tungsten film and you need to switch suddenly to daylight, it is possible to buy a conversion filter which corrects the otherwise heavy blue cast which would result. As a relatively strong filter is required for this, an appreciable increase in exposure is needed to compensate. Conversely of course a filter can be bought to convert daylight film for tungsten use. It is, however, preferable to use the correct film for the light source and these filters should be considered more as contingency measures rather than essential equipment.

Creating a colour cast has resulted in a more dramatic image, as these two pictures of autumn leaves on a pond illustrate. The top picture was shot without a filter. It is quite a pleasant photograph, but the photographer wanted the leaves to be a richer and redder tone than they appeared in his viewfinder. A 20 Magenta filter was used to achieve the second result (below) without any increase in exposure, simply a colour correction.

Problem

Correcting a colour cast is sometimes necessary when the light source does not match the balance of the film. Open shade is often a perfect light for portrait, but on colour film it can often produce a bluish cast, particularly when the sky is bright blue. If a blue or green tinge affects skin tones it can be very noticeable and distinctly unattractive, as the small picture shot without a filter demonstrates. The larger picture was taken with the addition of an 81B Wratten Filter, a light yellow filter with a touch of red. The filter was chosen by a combination of educated guesswork and experience. You can buy a colour temperature meter which measures the colour cast, but these are expensive and will probably not be used by the amateur photographer too frequently.

Lens attachments

Starburst attachments

Apart from colour filters there are a number of other devices which can be used in front of the camera lens to produce a range of interesting effects. Starburst filters, as their name implies, create streaks of light radiating from strong highlights. The effect will be more marked when the highlights are contrasted against dark background. The basic version provides four streaks at right angles; more elaborate versions include two filters which can be rotated to change the angles of the streaks in relation to each other.

Multiprisms

Prism lens attachments consist of a number of facets moulded into the surface which create repeat images within the picture area. A central image is usually surrounded by two or four repetitions which can be positioned by rotating the attachment. When used on a standard or wide angle camera lens the images are usually quite distinct and separate but when used with a slightly long lens the repeat images tend to merge and can be used to create almost abstract effects. Another version of this attachment creates the additional images either vertically or horizontally.

Split focus

This in effect is half a close-up lens. It enables the photographer to create the impression of tremendous depth of field. If the camera is focussed on the mid distance the addition of this device will bring into focus objects which are extremely close to the camera. As this attachment is actually a lens cut in half it must be positioned so that the distortion caused by the cut edge is disguised by some detail in the subject. By rotating the mount it can be adjusted to allow the close-up object to be positioned at either side or the top or bottom of the image area.

Apart from the specially manufactured devices that can be bought there are many other interesting ways of altering or distorting the image. Shooting through tumblers or wine glasses for example, through magnifying glasses and old spectacle lenses held in various positions in front of the camera lens, into reflective surfaces with distorted and textured surfaces, such as a polished steel tray, even breathing onto the surface of the camera lens to cause it to mist over, can create interesting effects. Under certain circumstances all of these tricks can add that extra quality to an image that lifts it out of the category of mere photography and into the realm of abstract art.

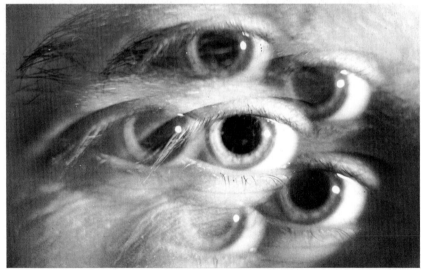

Starry raindrops (top) were created by pouring from a watering can and backlighting. The addition of a starburst filter has added a touch of magic to the picture.

The eyes have it and they were shot with the aid of a multi-prism.

A split focus attachment and a wide angle lens were necessary to achieve the great depth of field in the portrait (right).

Filters for dramatic colour

In recent years a number of colour effect filters have been developed which enable the photographer to introduce a degree of selective colour control into the image. Possibly the most useful of these is the graduated filter. This is simply a filter in which half is coloured and the other half clear with a gradual transition between the two sections. It enables the photographer to introduce a colour change into one half of the picture only, so that it is possible for example to add extra colour to a sunset without affecting the colour of the foreground in the bottom half of the picture. These filters can also be used vertically or at an angle so that they affect one side of the picture and not the other. They are available in a wide range of colours and various strengths, including neutral density, which is a grey filter and has no effect on the colour but can be used to darken one half of the image.

There are a number of derivations of this type of filter. One has clear glass in the centre and colour surrounding so that the centre of the picture remains unaffected by the colour introduced into the rest of the image. Another variation has two halves of different colours so that one can introduce, say, a yellow cast into one half of the picture and a blue cast into the other. The effects of these last two types of filter tend to be rather obvious unless used with great discretion, and they can easily produce rather gimmicky images.

The graduated filter used in the picture on the right has given considerable dramatic emphasis when compared with the unfiltered version on the left. In this instance a tobacco coloured strength 2 filter was used with no increase in exposure over the unfiltered exposure. This is important, as the purpose of the filter is not only to introduce colour into the selected area but also to increase density. It can be seen that the sky tones in the filtered version are much richer and intoned with more detail. In this picture the filter has been used to create an obviously unreal effect but the range of colours and densities available enables these devices to be used very subtly and to simply enhance the picture without drawing attention to their effect. The fact that a wide angle lens was used in these pictures has resulted in the colour change being quite well defined. A longer focal length lens would produce a more gradual effect.

The polarizing filter used in the right hand picture has produced two particularly noticeable effects. Firstly the sky has become a much darker and richer blue enabling the branches of the trees to be shown more dramatically. It can be seen from the tone of these trees that the relative overall exposure of the picture is the same in both examples, although a polarizing filter requires an exposure increase of approximately $1\frac{1}{2}$ stops to allow for its density. The second effect is that the filter has eliminated some of the light being reflected from the rocks and the palm tree leaves, resulting in a noticeable increase in colour quality. The effect of a polarizing filter is dependent on a number of factors, the angle of the light, the nature of the surfaces (it has no effect on reflections from metal surfaces) and the angle of rotation of the filter itself. Hold the filter can up to your eye and rotate it to judge whether it is worthwhile fitting to the camera lens.

Filters for black and white

Modern panchromatic black and white films record tones quite accurately regardless of colour so that a light red will record as a light grey and a dark blue as a dark grey and so on. There are occasions however, when you might wish to alter or emphasize certain tones in a picture. This can usually be achieved by the use of filters which are simply glass or plastic discs or squares of varying colours and densities which can be mounted in front of the camera lens. The effect that they have can be easily predicted. A coloured filter passes light from its own area of the spectrum freely but 'holds back' light of different colours. So a red filter will pass red, orange and yellow, but will hold back greens and blues. The result in the print is that the reds, oranges and yellows will appear lighter than they would without the filter and the greens and blues darker. The effect will vary according to the strength or density of the filter. A deep red filter for example, will record blue as a near black on the print, but a pale yellow will render it only a slightly darker grey than it would be without it. Because the filter is preventing some of the light from the subject passing through the camera lens, an increase in exposure will be required to produce an adequately exposed negative. The stronger the filter the greater the increase required. Most filters have a filter factor marked on them which indicate the increase needed. A (×2) factor represents a one stop increase, a (×4) two stops and so on.

Probably the most commonly used range of filters in black and white photography is the red to yellow range which is used primarily for increasing the tone of a blue sky and providing more contrast where there are white clouds. Because the sky is usually at the brighter end of the tonal range of the picture it can easily become devoid of detail and the use of a yellow filter will render a blue sky as a light grey enabling white clouds to be seen more clearly. A somewhat stronger and more dramatic effect can be produced by an orange filter, and with a red filter a deep blue sky will record as nearly black.

Colour filters can be used in black and white photography in a much wider context than simply darkening blue skies however and there are numerous occasions when the use of a filter can improve the tonal quality of a photograph. The texture of skin can be greatly enhanced in a 'character' portrait for example by using a deep blue filter. A red filter can be used to reduce the effect of skin blemishes. A green filter can be used in landscape photography to introduce lighter tones into large masses of dense green foliage. Filters can also be used to introduce contrast into a subject. If for example you were going to photograph a girl wearing a red shirt and blue jeans standing against a bright green door there would be a somewhat dramatic contrast in a colour shot but the same scene in a straight black and white picture would produce a flat all over mid grey image. A red filter, however, would produce a light shirt with a dark grey door and jeans, a green filter would produce a light door, a nearly black shirt and dark jeans, and a blue filter nearly white jeans a mid grey door and a dark grey shirt.

No filter was used for this picture of a girl wearing a red jumper, blue slacks and standing against a green background.

A green filter makes the red jumper record as near black, the green as near white and the slacks slightly darker.

A red filter results in the red jumper recording as near white, the blue slacks as near black, and the green darker.

A blue filter makes the blue trousers record as near white and the red jumper and green background as slightly darker.

Mist and haze in landscape photography can be minimized by the use of an orange or red filter with black and white film. These two pictures of the Atlas Mountains in Morocco quite clearly illustrate the effect that can be achieved. The picture right was shot with no filter and the distant mountains are rather indistinct. There is virtually no detail in the sky and the clouds are not visible. The picture above was taken only seconds later with a red filter, the distant mountains are now more clearly defined, the sky has become darker allowing the white clouds to be distinguished, and the snow on the mountain tops is more pronounced. There is also a greater variety of tones in the almond blossom trees in the foreground. Such a filter requires an increase of exposure, the filter used in the second picture was an X.8 requiring an exposure increase of 3 stops. This photograph was taken on a long lens and the effect of haze is increased when using such lenses.

Soft focus

This can be a most pleasing and effective technique when applied to the right subject. Most filter manufacturers supply soft focus attachments which range from a glass disc with concentric circles moulded into it to the more elaborate Zeiss Softar which has a number of minute bubbles embedded in it. However, the principle is the same. The irregularities in the surface of the attachment introduce flaws or aberrations into the performance of the lens, impairing its sharpness and diffusing the image it produces. This takes the 'edge' off the sharpness of the camera lens, which reduces the detail in the picture. At the same time, it causes the lighter areas of the subject to spread slightly into the shadows so lowering contrast and reducing colour saturation. Where very strong highlights are present, as in the hair of a backlit portrait, this effect can create an impression of luminosity.

Most soft focus attachments are available in various strengths and their effect can be further controlled by the aperture used. The smaller the aperture the lesser the effect. The effect is quite different and much more pleasant than that given by the image simply being 'out of focus', as with a soft focus attachment there is an underlying core of sharpness. Some attachments create softness only around the edges of the picture leaving the centre unaffected.

If you cannot afford the attachments, you can produce some very pleasing effects by using crumpled cellophane or strips of scotch tape stretched across the lens hood a few centimetres in front of the lens. Leave a clear area in the centre to permit the 'core' of sharpness. A UV filter, again with a clear spot in the centre, or vaseline smeared on to clear glass, is another way of achieving soft focus. The advantage of vaseline is that you can 'tease' it around with a finger tip to create a variety of streaks and blurring where there are strong highlights.

A Zeiss Softar mounted over the camera lens was used to shoot the two models above in Ibiza. This attachment can create particularly pleasant effects when combined with backlighting, as it makes the highlights to 'bleed' slightly into the darker tones creating a sort of halo effect. It can be bought in three strengths. The medium one was used for this picture. The overall effect will, however, depend on the aperture, the lighting and even the subject itself.

Scotch tape was used to produce the soft focus effect of the picture above. The comparison shot beside it shows clearly how the diffusion created by this technique affects the image. The shots were taken using a slightly long lens (150 mm on Pentax 6 × 7 cm) and a wide aperture was used to subdue background detail and to maximise the effect of the soft focus. Backlighting also contributes to the misty quality of the softened image and the exposure was calculated to record the face as a lightish tone.

A magnifying glass lens was used to shoot the woodland scene. It was fairly crudely mounted onto the camera (a Pentax 6 × 7 cm) with the aid of a cardboard tube and the camera's extension tube. The aperture was calculated by dividing the focal length of the lens by the diameter which produced a working aperture of f.3.3! Most of the soft focus techniques involved impairing the quality of a highly corrected (and expensive) lens and the effects achieved by using very cheap and very bad lenses can often be as good, if not better.

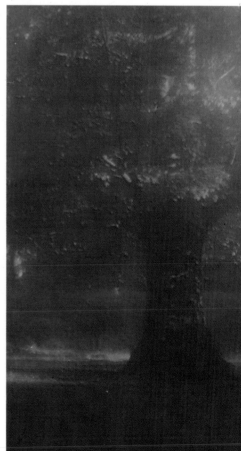

Fog filters

These filters are colourless but with a slightly milky appearance. They are usually supplied in two or three strengths. They introduce a degree of flare into the camera lens which does not affect sharpness but reduces contrast and colour saturation. They can be very effective in producing those slightly misty, romantic images with soft pastel colours, and can also be used to simply 'tone down' pictures where the colours are too strong and bright or the contrast too high. This effect like that of soft focus, is more pleasing and effective with colour materials, although it can be applied with some success to black and white work.

Diffraction gratings

These attachments, sometimes called colour burst filters, utilize the properties of diffraction to produce a nimbus of rainbow-coloured streaks radiating from bright highlights and reflections. As with starburst filters their effect is greatly enhanced when the background tones are predominately dark.

A fog filter was used to shoot the picture of Venice (above), on a winter evening. The lighting had already created a fairly soft image, but the fog filter has taken it just one stage further, and produced a quite delicate image. In this case it was used to exaggerate on existing effect, but a fog filter can also be used to reduce contrast where it is excessive.

The rainbow highlights radiating from the lady's high gloss fashion frock (left), were created by using a diffraction grating over the camera lens. Hard directional lighting was used to create really strong highlights, and a black background was chosen to enable the 'radiations' to show up strongly. These attachments are available with a variety of configurations and can be rotated to achieve the best effect.

Using close-up equipment

All but the most basic cameras are capable of being focussed down to about one metre. While this range enables subjects of about the size of a small animal like a cat to fill the frame it is simply not close enough to allow the photographer to explore a particularly interesting and satisfying area of photography.

Close-up lenses

These are positive lenses of various strengths which can be mounted in front of the camera lens to reduce its minimum focussing distance. As with anything used in the light path of the camera's optical system they will have an adverse effect on the performance of the camera lens. This can be minimized by stopping down to a small aperture. These lenses are usually sold with a chart showing how the camera lens focussing scale is affected, so that owners of simple cameras which do not have screen focussing can calculate the correct focus. Remember however that cameras with a separate viewfinder will cease to give an accurate indication of the field of view at distances of less than about two metres, so that at say half a metre the camera viewfinder will be very inaccurate. In these circumstances, you could make up a small frame which can be attached to the front of the camera showing the field of view at specific close distances. The field of view can be established by viewing through the back of the open camera (shutter open and close-up lens in position) with a piece of frosted acetate serving as a focussing screen.

Bellows and tubes

By far the most suitable type of camera for close-up work is the single lens reflex. The interchangeable lens and direct viewing and focussing system of this type of camera means that either a bellows unit or extension tubes can be introduced between the camera body and the camera lens, so dramatically increasing the close focussing range of the camera. Bellows and tubes both work on the same principle of moving the lens progressively further away from the film plane so that it will be able to focus on correspondingly closer objects.

Extension tubes are usually sold in sets of three different lengths and can be used either singly or in conjunction with each other. Many of them have a system which enables the camera lens to remain connected to the auto iris and open aperture metering systems of the camera body. Bellows extensions have the additional advantage of allowing an infinitely variable focussing range within its travel whereas the length of extension tubes restricts you to set stages.

Reversing rings

Because normal camera lenses are computed to give their best performance for normal situations where the lens-to-subject distance greatly exceeds its focal length, there will be some deterioration in its image quality when it is used at very close focus. You can overcome this effect to some extent by using a device called a reversing ring, which enables the lens to be used back to front.

A bellows unit affords a continuously variable degree of extension throughout its length. It is designed primarily for use with SLR cameras.

A ring flash (top right) is mounted on the camera lens and provides a shadowless light of considerable intensity. It is ideal for illuminating close-up subjects where a maximum amount of detail is required. The very short flash exposure makes hand held camera operation possible.

Extension Tubes (right) offer a less variable control of extension than a bellows unit but are usually cheaper. Normally sold in sets of three different lengths, they can be mounted individually or together between the camera body and lens. They are suitable only for SLR.

Macro and close focussing lenses

Close-up photography is where the object appears smaller than life size on the film and macro photography is when the image is enlarged beyond 1:1, or life size. Many lenses are now available that can double as a normal lens and a close focus or macro lens. Such a lens has the advantage of being a complete unit needing no further attachments, and retaining all the facilities, such as open aperture metering and auto iris control, possessed by the camera body itself.

When working at very close distances where the subject to image ratio is around 1:1, the depth of focus will be very shallow indeed and a small aperture will be necessary to ensure adequate detail in the picture. You will also find that the slightest movement will cause the focus to shift dramatically and good firm tripod is essential for the most critical work. When shooting close-ups out of doors *in situ*, a flower for example, the slightest movement will cause serious loss of definition with all but the shortest exposures. It is a good idea to make a small, portable screen from card or hardboard to protect such subjects from breezes.

Calculating exposure

When the lens is moved appreciably further away from the film plane, the exposure has to be increased correspondingly to compensate for the resulting decrease in brightness on the film. The increase of exposure is minimal until the lens is extended beyond about ten percent of its focal length. A camera with TTL or automatic metering will measure the decrease in illumination at the film plane so a calculation will be unnecessary, but photographers using a separate exposure meter or flash will need to make a simple calculation. The brightness of the image decreases in direct proportion to the distance the lens is moved beyond its focal length. The exposure increase can be calculated by dividing the square of the distance of the lens from the film plane by the square of the focal length of the lens. For example, a 5 cm lens extended to 10 cm will require four times the indicated exposure ($\frac{100}{25} = 4$).

Where the lens extension cannot be measured easily, as in the case of a close-up lens attachment or a macro lens, the exposure increase

A close-up lens on a simple camera can be used to take pictures like this shot of a rusty latch on a wooden gate. Close-up lenses are simply positive lenses of various strengths which can be mounted on the front of the camera lens like a filter. They allow the focussing range of the camera lens to be extended well beyond its normal closest distance depending on the strength of the attachment. A small aperture should be used to obtain the best definition.

Chart for exposure increase with lens extension in closeup work
(Based on a basic exposure of 1 second)

Extension as a percentage	Extension with a 50 mm lens	Exposure
0 %	50 mm	1 sec
10 %	55 mm	1·2 sec
20 %	60 mm	1·4 sec
30 %	65 mm	1·7 sec
40 %	70 mm	2 secs
50 %	75 mm	2·3 secs
60 %	80 mm	2·6 secs
70 %	85 mm	2·9 secs
80 %	90 mm	3·2 secs
90 %	95 mm	3·6 secs
100 %	100 mm	4 secs
110 %	110 mm	4·8 secs
120 %	120 mm	5·8 secs
130 %	130 mm	6·8 secs
140 %	140 mm	7·8 secs
150 %	150 mm	9 secs

can be calculated by the ratio between the image size and the size of the subject. To compute the required increase, divide the size of the image by the size of the subject, add one and then square the result. For example, if the subject is 2 cm high and the image 1 cm high the calculation is:

$$(\tfrac{1}{2}+1)^2 = \tfrac{3}{2} \times \tfrac{3}{2} = \tfrac{9}{4} = 2.25$$

Using ring flash

There are a number of factors which can make the lighting of close-up subjects something of a problem. The small apertures and increases of exposures for extension mean that either a bright light source or quite long exposures are required. An additional consideration is that at very close distances the lens is so close to the subject that it can make it difficult to actually get the light in there. While long exposures can be the solution for some subjects, there are many where it is simply not possible.

An answer to this problem is the ring flash. This is an electronic flash tube moulded into a circle and fitted into a mount which screws onto the filter ring of the camera lens. It is powered from a separate power pack so that the actual light source (the flash tube) is extremely light and compact. It has the obvious advantage of being able to move as close to the subject as the lens itself, so that as the lens is extended the illumination increases correspondingly. Furthermore as the light source surrounds the lens, the resulting lighting effect is virtually shadowless, so that with very close-up subjects the maximum possible detail can be recorded.

A ring flash was used to illuminate this picture of a gnarled piece of wood. The fine detail is revealed by the virtually shadowless lighting provided by this accessory. Using flash lighting means that a small aperture may be used, which also eliminates the possibility of movement. This results in a picture with superb definition. This type of image needs to be as sharp as possible and using ring flash can be a useful method not only of illumination but also of ensuring a sharp picture, it was shot on a macro lens.

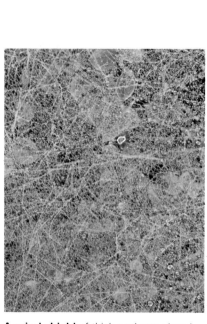

A wind shield of thick card was placed around this fine tracery of cobwebs to protect it from draughts. The camera was mounted on a tripod to enable an exposure of one second to be given and the macro lens was stopped down to f.16 to ensure adequate depth of field.

An extension tube was used in conjunction with a 105 mm lens to shoot this picture of early morning dew. A fairly wide aperture was used to allow the backlit droplets of water in the background to create a shimmering quality. The purpose of many close-up pictures is to convey as much information as possible and overall sharpness is an undoubted advantage in these cases, but the possibility of creating purely pictorial effects with close-up pictures is well worth exploring. It can be a rewarding field of photography, even if you are not scientifically motivated.

Hand held exposures are quite workable in close-up photography providing there is a reasonably bright source of light. With pictures like this shot of a butterfly it is almost essential to hand hold in order to follow the insect and frame the picture quickly as soon as it settles. Using flash can be an advantage but this shot was taken with available light. It was possible to use a fast shutter speed as little depth of field was required and a fairly wide aperture could be used. In this picture a shallow depth of field has helped to isolate the subject from its background.

A macro lens was used to produce this image of a small section of an Abalone shell. It was taken with window light indoors, the camera mounted on a tripod with an exposure of one second at about f.16. A small white card reflector was used close to the surface of the shell to create additional highlights. This is a good example of how close-up photography of relatively commonplace objects can be used to create almost abstract pictures. With the addition of a relatively inexpensive accessory to your equipment such as a close-up lens or an extension tube, it is possible to greatly extend the range of your subject matter.

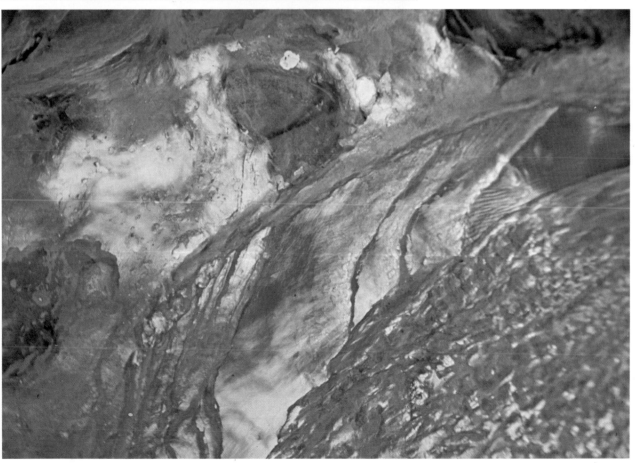

103

USING LENSES

The standard lens which is normally supplied with a camera is good for most shots. It has an angle of view which is wide enough for a high percentage of subjects but still provides a reasonably large image of distant scenes. It is nevertheless a compromise, and the acquisition of one or more lenses of a narrower or wider angle of view will enable a photographer to develop a new approach, to create quite different images and to produce successful pictures in situations where a standard lens would be quite impossible.

Wide angle lens

A lens is considered to be wide angle when it offers a field of view wider than about 60°. Its most obvious effect is to reduce the size of the image in the viewfinder. At the same time it allows objects in the foreground to be included which a normal lens would exclude. Obviously the wider the angle the greater these effects. Apart from these facilities, a wide angle lens offers other, less obvious advantages. It has a greater depth of field than longer lenses, and by including more of the foreground area it exaggerates perspective and increases the feeling of depth in a picture.

There are also a number of disadvantages to this piece of equipment that you should bear in mind. Its greater depth of field means that in normal circumstances there is a tendency for pictures to be sharp all over, so that more care is needed in isolating the main centre of interest. It is much easier to produce pictures which are 'busy' and confusing with this type of lens.

The inclusion of more foreground without the necessity of moving further back also means that there is a considerable risk of perspectives being so greatly exaggerated that they appear distorted. This can be particularly apparent when photographing subjects well endowed with parallel vertical lines, such as architecture. As soon as the camera is tilted up or down away from the horizontal the lines will begin to converge. This occurs regardless of which lens is used, but the closer viewpoint of the wide angle exaggerates the effect dramatically. Perspective is purely a function of viewpoint and is not related to the focal length of the lens, with the exception of specially computed lenses such as fisheye and anamorphic. As with most 'faults' that exist in the photographic process, these effects can be used intentionally to produce unusual and dramatic images but if they are caused without deliberate intention the result is usually unpleasant and distracting.

Dramatic perspective and a great depth of field are two qualities which have been fully exploited in this picture of Deal pier. A 20 mm lens and a small aperture were used in this shot. The exaggerated perspective has been used boldly.

105

Landscape

It is the particular ability to create a strong impression of depth that makes the wide angle lens a specially useful tool for the landscape photographer. By including close foreground areas in the picture area and enhancing the impression of perspective, the wide angle lens offers a unique quality to this area of photography. Remember that while the effect of a longer lens can be obtained by enlarging or cropping, there is no way of creating wide angle effects without using a wide angle lens.

In addition to including more foreground area the wide angle lens will also of course allow more sky area to be shown. This is particularly useful when a dramatic or interesting sky is an important element in the composition of a picture. The effect of polarizing and special effect filters will be much stronger in such pictures when used with a wide angle lens.

Another advantage of these lenses, particularly valuable in landscape work, is that it needs only a slight change of viewpoint to achieve a marked variation on the composition and the juxtaposition of the elements in the picture. As well as lateral changes in viewpoint, the wide angle lens can be especially effective when working from a low or high position, creating much more dramatic results than would be achieved with lenses of longer focal length.

When a bright sun is included in the picture the effect tends to be more pleasing with a wide angle lens, which often causes 'starburst' type streaks to radiate from it, eliminating the need for attachments. With the wide angle, flare is less likely to occur and consequently it is easier to maintain the contrast of the subject when shooting into the sun than when longer lenses are used.

A dramatic sky is often enhanced by the use of a wide angle lens. This picture (left) taken in the Swiss alps was shot on a 55 mm lens and its impact is partly due to the exaggerated perspective effect created by the lens.

The fine detail which was required into the extreme corners of the picture of autumn leaves (top), was ensured by the use of a small aperture and a 20 mm lens.

A close foreground is often required in landscape photography to help create a feeling of depth. The picture above was shot on a 24 mm lens and although the light level required a fairly wide aperture the foreground is still adequately sharp.

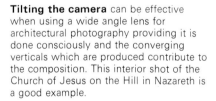

Tilting the camera can be effective when using a wide angle lens for architectural photography providing it is done consciously and the converging verticals which are produced contribute to the composition. This interior shot of the Church of Jesus on the Hill in Nazareth is a good example.

Filling the foreground is often necessary when a wide angle lens is used and the camera is not tilted upwards, because although it keeps the verticals parallel it often creates an empty space at the bottom of the frame. Two children and their goats have provided the necessary interest in this shot of David's Tower in Jerusalem.

Architecture
Wide angle lenses are particularly useful in architectural photography because they are able to include more of the subject matter without the photographer having to move further back. This applies equally to interiors and exteriors of buildings. In many situations the viewpoints of a particular building are usually quite limited and often it is only by using a wide angle lens that all the major parts of a building can be included in the frame.

The main problem is the effect of tilting the camera, which greatly exaggerates the perspective effect of verticals. The solution is either to use the converging verticals in a way which contributes to the mood and composition of a picture, or not to tilt it at all.

There are three ways to avoid tilting the camera in order to include the top of a building in the picture. Most obvious (but not always possible) is to move further back. This will inevitably include more foreground area than you might have wanted. This can be overcome by simply cropping off the surplus area or by finding some foreground interest that can be used as an additional element in the composition. If space is so restricted that you cannot move further back then try moving the camera position higher. Often it is possible to gain access to a building opposite the one you wish to photograph and to shoot from a position about halfway up the face of your subject.

The only other alternative is to use a lens or a camera which enables the optical axis of the lens to be moved higher in relation to the film. This lets you raise the viewpoint optically without having to actually move the camera higher. Most large format view or technical cameras have this facility, which explains why they are widely used by professional architectural photographers. However, a number of lens manufacturers make 'perspective control lenses' designed to fit single lens reflex cameras. These are simply wide angle lenses fitted to a panel, with a screw adjustment which allows the lens to be shifted away from the optical axis. The panel can be rotated so that the lens can be moved horizontally as well as vertically.

If none of these alternatives are possible, then the only way to include the top of a tall building is to go ahead and tilt the camera upwards. If this is done in a considered way the result can be extremely effective. As a general rule, if you stand in a position opposite and in the centre of the base of the building you are shooting, and tilt the camera so that the base of the building is included in the picture, the result is usually a photograph of a building about to fall backwards. You can avoid this effect in a number of ways. First of all, exclude the base of the building. Secondly don't allow the picture to become too symmetrical, stand towards one corner rather than in the centre; it can also be helpful to allow some foreground detail to appear in the top or sides of the frame, for instance an overhanging branch or an archway. A more pleasing effect can often be gained by tilting the

A low viewpoint can be exploited more dramatically when using a wide angle lens as this picture of the Eiffel Tower demonstrates. The lens used here was a 20 mm and the picture taken from the base of the tower. It would simply not have been possible to have shot from this position and to have included both the arches and the top of the tower without such a lens.

Great depth of field and enhanced perspective are the qualities for which the 24 mm lens was chosen to shoot this picture of champagne bottles being turned to dislodge their sediment. Relatively low light meant that a fairly wide aperture had to be used, but the depth of field is still quite adequate for the job. The viewpoint allowed by a wide angle lens has created a strong diagonal.

camera horizontally as well as vertically. These camera angles are usually more effective when there is some detail or interest in the sky tone, such as strong white clouds or even just a rich blue sky. As a final generalization it is better to overdo the effect of tilting rather than to approach it too tentatively and allow it to simply look like a fault.

Reportage photography

Whenever you are shooting in situations where there is movement, excitement, crowds of people and lots of activity the wide angle lens can be a vital accessory. A quick glance through the news magazines will show that such a lens is a popular, almost obligatory choice for today's photojournalists. It can however be just as useful for the man who wants to photograph a childrens' tea party as it is for someone covering a demonstration.

In crowd conditions, the considerable depth of field and lack of need for critical focussing which is inherent in a wide angle lens is high on the list of advantages. It is possible to change angles and viewpoints quickly to follow the movement of the action without the encumbrance of a swiftly changing plane of focus. The ability to work at close quarters to your subject and still include a wide field of view creates a quality of involvement and intimacy in the pictures which in turn gives the viewer a much stronger impression of reality.

A less obvious advantage of these lenses is that they enable a photographer to work close in to his subject without anyone realizing that they *are* the subject, especially as the lens often does not need to be pointed directly at them. Inexperienced photographers may well believe that a long lens is much more useful for candid photography but this is by no means necessarily so, and in many circumstances a wide angle lens is far less likely to attract the subject's attention.

A sense of involvement is created by the close viewpoint afforded by the use of a 24 mm lens in this picture of children in a school playground.

A confusing image can easily result when a wide angle lens is used because almost everything is sharp. Careful composition and viewpoint is necessary to avoid this, and although a busy image was intended in this picture taken in Tel Aviv's Flea Market, the old lady still becomes the focus of attention.

The long lens

There is no doubt that a long lens can give a photographer a sense of power. To be able to reach forward into space and pluck subjects out of thin air is certainly a feeling that comes with the first glance through a really long lens. Used in conjunction with a perceptive eye and a good sense of composition such a lens can be a powerful tool. Of course the most obvious effect is the enlargement of the image but an immediate result of this is the reduction in depth and the impression of perspective that goes with the more distant viewpoints used with these lenses. This requires a rather different approach to composition, as pictures taken with a long lens are more two dimensional with the emphasis laying more on shapes and less on form. Because a more distant viewpoint can be used, it is possible to tilt the camera up at a building without the resulting perspective effect being as noticeable. The more subtle effect on perspective also makes a slightly long lens useful for portraiture since it enables the image of a face to adequately fill the frame without the need for a close viewpoint. Anything closer than about two metres will result in discernible distortion of facial features.

The depth of field is much shallower with a long lens and focussing needs to be critically accurate. Out of focus areas become more positive and selective focussing effects are much more dramatic with a longer lens.

One disadvantage with these lenses is that because they magnify the image they are much more vulnerable to subject and camera movement than shorter lenses. To insure maximum image sharpness you must either use high shutter speeds or have the camera firmly supported, either on a tripod or held against some natural support such as a tree or a wall. This is further complicated by the fact that most long lenses are slower than standard ones with smaller maximum apertures and often a faster film becomes necessary in all but the best lighting conditions.

Sport and nature photography
The long lens is particularly suitable for subjects which cannot be approached closely and when a more distant viewpoint is forced upon the photographer. Such a lens is considered as standard equipment by both sport and nature photographers. Both subjects present much the same sort of technical problem to the photographer, whether he is shooting from a hide in the woods or the grandstand of a football stadium. Supporting the camera and minimizing the effects of movement is a prime consideration and while a good firm tripod is perhaps the most satisfactory answer, anything which increases the stability of the camera is worth using. Sports photographers often use camera supports with a rifle

Shallow depth of field as a result of shooting with a 200 mm lens at its widest aperture of f.3.5 has isolated the main subject of this picture taken in a Marrakesh street. Although the foreground is quite busy, it has not been allowed to detract from the subject because the area of sharp focus has not extended that far. The more distant viewpoint afforded by the use of a long lens has enabled the photographer to back away from the scene and then literally reach forward with the lens and scoop his picture out of the crowd. Low light level and a moving subject required a fairly fast shutter speed. The film used was Ektachrome 200.

Isolating a small area of a scene is one of the facilities that a long lens offers. The picture of a setting sun was taken on a 300 mm lens and represents only a small area of the scene. The light level was quite low. Shot on Kodachrome 64, it needed an exposure of 1/125 second at the lens's maximum aperture of f.4.5. It would be easy to get camera shake at this speed, and as no tripod was available great care was needed.

The compressed planes of perspective apparent in this shot of Sunday strollers in an English park is the result of shooting with a 600 mm lens. It is sometimes called a distorted perspective but this is not really so. It is simply that we are not accustomed to seeing such distant subjects in close-up and if it were possible to enlarge the same small portion of the scene taken on a standard lens the perspective effect would be identical.

No impression of depth is often the result of pictures taken on a long lens because a distant viewpoint creates little difference in perspective. The shot (above) of Port Talbot in South Wales was taken on a 300 mm lens and appears to be virtually on one plane. This, combined with a limited tonal range has produced an image with no depth or form. It is entirely dependent on design for its impact.

Getting closer is sometimes just not possible. A long lens was used to obtain a relatively 'close-up' picture of this bull fight in Barcelona's Plaza de Torros. A lens of 200 mm or more is very useful for any form of spectator sport where the photographer is not able to get close to the subject.

Taking animal portraits can add a great deal of pleasure to a visit to the zoo. A long lens lets you take close-up pictures such as the shot of the elephant (above right), and to remove any impression of the bars and cages. Both animal pictures were taken on a 200 mm lens.

butt handle, which can be tucked into the shoulder, and a trigger to fire the shutter connected by a cable release. Other useful devices are monopods and chestpods both of which enable the camera to be pushed down against a support. Lacking any of these, hold the camera in such a way that it can be braced against the body with the elbows and upper arms, if it is an eye-level camera. If it has a waist level viewfinder, press if firmly against the chest.

The shallow depth of field is something which can be used to advantage by sport and nature photographers, as the highly selective

The zoo offers many interesting animal subjects, such as this seal.

113

plane of focus is an invaluable aid to isolating the subject from its background and subduing fussy and irrelevant details. Another advantage of the shallow depth of field is the loss of foreground detail. This can be very useful when shooting pictures of animals behind bars and wires. By getting the camera as close as possible to the wires and using a fairly wide aperture when focussing on the subject, the cage will become undetectable in the photograph. When photographing domestic and farm animals a longer lens enables the photographer to work at a distance which allows the animal to be less aware of his presence and thus behave more naturally. This 'convenient' working distance can also be useful with close-up subjects where a shorter lens would necessitate the camera being almost on top of the subject, in botanical photography for example.

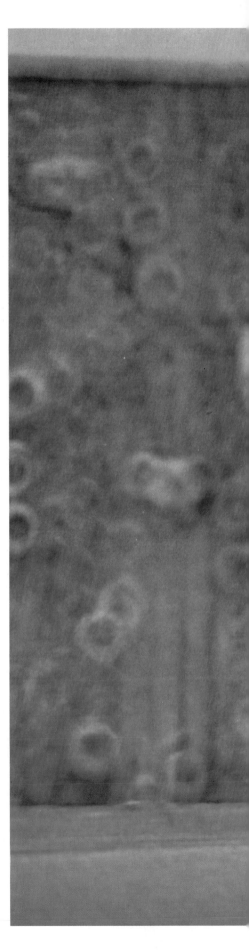

Subduing unwanted background detail is made relatively easy with a long lens. This posed shot of the cat (above) taken in a garden has successfully separated the subject from its background.

Timid animals in the wild often cannot be approached closely enough to produce a large enough image and the use of a long lens can make all the difference.

Prefocussing and anticipation are needed to produce crisp, close-up pictures like this dramatic shot of Barry Sheene cornering at Brands Hatch, Kent. The trick is to select the spot where the action is going to be, prefocus on the ground, preferably finding a mark which you can identify, and then frame the picture and wait until your subject appears in the viewfinder.

Special effects

Lenses over about 200 mm used on 35 mm film can give quite dramatic and unusual effects. This is largely due to the apparent compression of perspective which occurs from distant viewpoints. The lens does not create this compression, it simply allows us to see it more readily.

When we look at a distant view we tend to see it in the context of its surroundings and foreground, and when we take a picture with a very long lens we are simply taking a distant scene out of its context. This makes it seem unusual, but in fact if you were to enlarge that section of the picture from a photograph taken on a normal lens the perspective effect would be precisely the same. It is nonetheless a technique which has produced some remarkable and stunning images. It

works best when two or more objects are presented in such a way that their relative scale in the picture introduces an element of surprise.

Two classic examples of this are the big red sun shot on perhaps a 1000 mm lens with say a silhouetted church steeple in front of it. In some strange way we are surprised to see the sun as large as that, although of course it always is, it's simply that we have taken it out of context and we don't go around comparing it with church steeples all the time. The other standard eye stopper is the tiny silhouetted fishing boat on a vast sea dwarfed by a huge cliff or mountain. We all know that cliffs and mountains are considerably larger than fishing boats but for once we have been forced to see it in an unfamiliar way.

Apart from the relative scale of the objects in the picture, it is also the almost non-existence of depth and perspective in photographs taken on very long lenses that help to create an unusual effect. In these pictures the possibility of creating an illusion of three dimensions is relinquished and we begin to see and present images which exist only in two dimensions. Such photographs become almost entirely dependent on the juxtaposition of objects and their relative shapes, and composition becomes more concerned with shape than form.

Lenses of 500 mm or more focal length become very bulky and quite heavy and their relatively large degree of magnification means a greatly increased risk of camera shake. The minimum practicable shutter speed for hand held shots

A zoom lens was used to produce the effect of this shot of a racing car. It was taken by framing and focussing on the car with the zoom at its longest setting, in this case 200 mm and then with a longish shutter speed of 1/15 second, sharply but smoothly pulling the zoom back to its shortest length of 80 mm. The effect is greater towards the edges and corners of the picture and it works best when there is a good contrast between the tones in the picture.

A mirror lens has produced these characteristic circular spots on the out of focus highlights in the background of this picture of a song thrush. These lenses have a fixed aperture, in this case f.8, and the exposure can only be controlled by varying the shutter speed. As the depth of field can not be increased by stopping down as with normal lenses focussing becomes very critical. They do have the advantage of being much more compact and more easy to hold than the equivalent focal length lens of normal design.

should be 1/500 second, and hand holding should be a last resort. A rigid tripod is vital for this type of photography.

The mirror lens is an exception to the normal bulk and weight of very long lenses. Their compact design and lack of heavy glass components make them much more manageable and portable than conventional telephotos. Their drawback is that they have a fixed aperture of usually f.8 or f.11 and the exposure must be controlled by shutter speed alone.

The zoom lens
This has been one of the most significant of recent innovations. Designed originally for the motion picture industry, zooms have now become an important part of the still photographer's range of equip-

ment. Their most obvious advantage is that of convenience. At the present time the whole range of focal lengths from 25 mm to 300 mm can be carried in only three objectives. They are admittedly bulkier and heavier than conventionally designed lenses, and the cheaper versions cannot match the definition and image contrast of fixed focal length lenses, but a good quality zoom lens can be a very valuable and effective accessory.

Their greatest facility is that they eliminate compromise when it comes to framing the image. Normally you would have to decide between say the 85 mm and the 200 mm, when something in between would give a better crop, but with a 70 mm to 210 mm zoom you can adjust the framing infinitely.

Another advantage is that where

there is a degree of subject movement, as in a football match, the zoom can be adjusted to keep the image suitably framed without the operator moving. The zoom lens also creates another opportunity for a photographer to add the impression of movement to action shots. With relatively slow shutter speeds, the zoom can be used during the exposure either instead of or in addition to panning with a moving subject.

This effect can also be used with stationary subjects. With the camera mounted on a tripod and the zoom on its longest setting, and by exposing at say 1/2 sec. and simultaneously moving the zoom smoothly back to its shortest setting, you will get blurred streaks radiating from the centre of the image to the corners of the picture.

MAKING MULTIPLE IMAGES

Many of the techniques which have developed in photography are the result of photographers wanting to create something more than just a record of the subjects they shoot, wanting to produce images which become more of a personal expression and less of a factual representation. The technique of combining two or more images onto the same piece of film offers photographers the opportunity of moving as far away as possible from a literal representation.

The surrealistic seascape was created by sandwiching two transparencies of the same scene, but with one upside down and laterally reversed, and also half a stop lighter.

Back projection is one way of building a composite image. The dominant dice were a figment of photographic imagination, not a gambler's nightmare.

Double exposure

This is the most basic of the multiple image techniques, and used creatively can be one of the most effective. The main requirement is a camera which allows two exposures to be made without advancing the film. It is possible to run the film through the camera twice after carefully marking the starting position, but this is a troublesome and not entirely accurate method.

The most important thing to remember when making two or more exposures on the same piece of film, is that each of the exposures must be reduced, otherwise the result will be overexposed. In general terms, if two exposures are to be made, then the calculated exposures should be halved, and with three, one third of each exposure should be given. In practical terms, however it is usually more effective when one of the images dominates the other. If, for example, you wished to make a montage using the image of a landscape scene and one of a brick wall, and the two exposures were equally balanced, the resulting image may well be confusing and ineffective. In this situation it would be preferable to allow one of the images to dominate by reducing the exposure of the other image more.

You can also control the relative importance of the component images with colour filters. By using a blue filter for one image and a yellow for the other, for example, it is possible to impose a marked separation. Another possibility is to use focus. If you shoot one of the images out of focus, the other will quite naturally have more impact.

The relative distribution of the tones in each image is also a very important factor. If one of the images has an area of sky then this will effectively obliterate any subsequent exposure in that area. What is really happening when you make a double exposure is that the unused or partly used (dark) areas of the film are being used again on the second or subsequent exposures and areas that have been virtually 'used up' in the first exposure (bright tones) are no longer available to record a second image. With some cameras that have accessible viewing screens, the Hasselblad for example, it is useful to make a tracing of the first subject on a piece of film taped onto the screen. This will help you position other images accurately.

The slide copier

One of the problems with double or multiple exposure is that often the two subjects you want to montage are not available at the same time or even in the same place. You may have to make one of the exposures and then wait hours or even days before being able to make the second exposure.

A slide copier is a very useful accessory for those who are interested in making multiple images, because it enables the component images to be recorded separately and then combined later at leisure. Recollated in tranquillity, as it were. The basic principles still apply, but you have much greater freedom in selecting and combining the subjects. It can of course be a great deal easier to evaluate the images and to decide how best to superimpose them when you actually have the transparencies before you.

The slide copier also allows a further technique which is not possible with the camera alone. This is the 'sandwich', where two (or more) transparencies are sandwiched together and then rephotographed with the aid of the copier. The effect is quite different to that of double exposure, because with the sandwich the images are being added together and with double exposure one is, in effect, being subtracted from the other. This method also has the advantage of giving you a perfectly accurate prediction of the result. You simply look at the combined transparencies.

Using projectors

A slide projector can also be used most effectively to produce multiple image effects. With just one projector it is possible to project a preselected transparency directly onto another subject. This can be done either with or without additional lighting. If the projected image is the sole source of illumination then it is only the outline or the shapes and tones within the object which will become the second element of the image. The projector can be used from a position in line with the camera viewpoint or it can be used from a more oblique angle which will introduce shadows into the subject. If additional lighting is used it must be carefully balanced to the level of illumination given by the projected image, as this can easily be 'drowned'. Often only back or strong side lighting is used, as this leaves large areas of dark shadow to be illuminated by the projected image. If you are shooting in colour, use film which is balanced for the light source of the projector.

If two or more projectors are available then it becomes possible to produce more complicated images. By lining up the projectors with their preselected transparencies, the images can be positioned and superimposed on a piece of white card and the result can be viewed through the camera. But unlike a basic double exposure, a very useful additional control becomes available. Small discs of

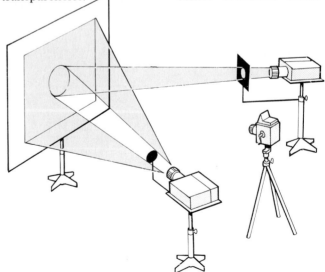

Montaging with projectors needs one projector for each image. Project one transparency from the first projector onto the screen, masking out the unwanted area. Project the second image, again with the unwanted area masked off, to fill the 'hole' on the screen. Make the exposure, keeping the room dark. Use film balanced for the light source of the projectors when making such montages.

card, and larger pieces with holes cut out can be supported on pieces of wire in front of the projector lenses (about a quarter of the distance between them and the screen). Selected areas of the projected images can then be erased and by carefully registering the positions of the shading devices you can blend the images together almost imperceptibly. You can also move the projectors to alter the relative scale of the images, and as with normal double exposures, colour filters can also be introduced selectively if required.

The opportunities offered by this technique are almost limitless. It is also possible to build up multiple images with only one projector and a series of exposures on the same piece of film, using a tracing as a position guide on the camera or position screen, but it is not possible to preview the result.

Back projection
This technique enables a projected transparency to be used as a background to a still-life arrangement. You need a frame, covered with a fine grain tracing paper, large enough to cover the background area of the still-life. This is positioned immediately behind the still-life. Then you set up your projector behind the screen facing towards the camera and size up and focus the selected background transparency. The still-life should be lit and composed in the normal way with the camera mounted on a firm tripod. When all is ready the screen must be covered with a black non-reflective fabric—velvet is ideal—and then with the still-life lighting on, the calculated exposure is given. Don't move anything now except the black fabric if necessary. With the screen and its projected image now exposed and *all other lighting* extinguished (a darkened room is essential) a second exposure calculated for the projected image is made on the same piece of film.

The resulting transparency will show both images, and if nothing has moved they will be in perfect alignment. You will have to cover or disguise the join between the surface upon which the still-life is arranged and the edge of the projection screen but this can usually be done quite subtly when arranging the still-life.

Front projection
The problem with back projection

Back projection means making two exposures onto the same piece of film, so is no good for subjects that are likely to move. Set up a projector directly in line with the camera. Assemble and light the still-life. Erect a frosted screen behind the still-life and project the transparency onto it. Cover the screen with non-reflective black fabric. Make the exposure of the still-life as normal. Remove the black cloth, switch out all the lights and make a second exposure to record the back-projected transparency.

is that because two separate exposures are necessary, the technique has to be restricted to subjects with a static foreground. It would not be possible to use this method to provide a background to a portrait, for example, as the slightest movement on the part of the model would create a distinct 'rim' around the head and give the game away.

When shooting with models it is necessary to use front projection. With an angled two-way mirror in front of the camera lens, the projector beams the background transparency along the optical axis of the camera. A highly reflective screen with a specially directional surface positioned behind the model reflects this image straight back into the camera lens. The projector is illuminated during the exposure with electronic flash and this, combined with the brilliant screen, allows the model to be lit normally and one simultaneous exposure made of both model and projected image.

The screen must be shielded from any stray light used to illuminate the model, and it is of course vital that this lighting should be balanced to match the brightness of the projected image. This type of equipment is used in professional studios and enables models to be photographed against exotic backgrounds without the 'inconvenience' of actually having to leave the studio. A simpler (and smaller) version of this equipment is available for the keen amateur to provide a limitless variety of backgrounds.

Using mirrors
A much simpler but nonetheless effective method of producing a secondary image is by using a mirror, or anything with a highly reflective surface. A simple pocket mirror can be used, held or supported immediately in front of the camera lens. A single lens reflex is essential for this technique, as it is necessary to view through the lens while positioning the mirror. The effect will alter dramatically with the smallest change of position or angle of the mirror. By holding it in the centre of the lens *almost* in line with the optical axis you will get a repeat or mirror image of one half of the picture. By increasing the angle of the mirror away from the axis, you can superimpose images from outside the camera's view onto the image at which the camera is aimed. The possibilities and variety of effects can be increased by using a flexible mirror which can be rolled into a tube (with the mirror surface on the inside) and shooting through this. Three rigid mirrors can be used to shoot through in kaleidoscope fashion and additional impact can be gained by using coloured gelatines on the surface of one or more of the mirrors.

It is also possible to create abstractions by shooting into found reflective surfaces such as windows or puddles. Keep your eyes and mind open to alternative ways of presenting an image and develop a personal touch.

A subtle blend of two images was produced in the montage above, using two projectors and two transparencies, a close-up of an abalone shell and a close-up of a woman's breast.

A simple reflection in a window provided the distorted image of a boat (left). To be successful, this type of photograph requires the object being reflected to be lit much more strongly than the surface in which it is reflected.

One projector was used to superimpose a seascape directly onto the head of the model in the dream picture (above right).

Double exposure was used to achieve the effect of mingled leaves and grass (right). The background exposure was given proportionately slightly less time than that of the leaves.

ARTIFICIAL LIGHT

To be able to control and exploit the use of artificial light will greatly extend the scope of your photography. There are many situations where daylight is either inadequate, unsuitable or simply inconvenient. Knowing how to use artificial lighting will enable you to tackle any situation, regardless of lighting conditions, from highly controllable studio lighting to illuminated buildings at night.

There are two basic options when it comes to choosing studio lighting: tungsten or electronic flash. Tungsten lighting involves less expense, in fact a practical person could more or less build his own. All that is really required is a number of stands or supports with lamp holders and reflectors mounted on them so their position and angle can be altered easily. While the varied and sophisticated range of reflectors and attachments that are provided with manufactured equipment are very nice to have and convenient to use, it is surprising what you can do with just a number of basic light sources. The main disadvantages with tungsten lighting is, firstly, the degree of heat they generate. It can be very uncomfortable for a model to be surrounded by it. Also the filament lamps used in tungsten lighting gradually deteriorate and there can be a significant change in colour quality, which makes it more difficult to produce constant and predictable results. Secondly, when working in colour you will need to use a specially balanced film and it is not easy to switch quickly from daylight to tungsten.

Electronic flash
This has become the standard form of lighting in most professional studios and it does offer some definite advantages. First of all because the exposures are made by flash the 'modelling lights', which are provided to enable the lamps to be positioned, need be only of normal brightness and the model is not subjected to a constant glare. Secondly, because the actual exposure is made by an extremely brief flash, the problem of subject or camera movement is virtually eliminated and it is possible to obtain the maximum possible definition from a lens. A third advantage is that the colour quality and output of a flash tube is more constant than that of tungsten lamps and results are consequently more predictable. The

colour temperature of the flash tubes match that of daylight balanced film and different film. It is of course possible to mix electronic flash with daylight.

Cost is a possible disadvantage, but a modest studio electronic flash outfit can be bought for the price of a new lens. Another disadvantage is that with electronic flash exposure is determined by the power of the flash, the distance it is from the subject and the aperture used, so that a low powered flash outfit can restrict its working distance, and/or the choice of aperture. This can be a particular problem with still-life photography where small apertures are often needed to get maximum depth of field.

An ordinary exposure meter cannot be used for calculating flash exposures as they are too brief. You can buy a special flash meter or calculate exposures by the guide number method. Manufacturers of flash equipment supply a guide number which relates to the output of a particular unit and a specific film speed. The exposure is calculated by dividing the distance of the flash from the subject into this number and the result is the aperture required. Film of a different speed can be allowed for by adjusting the aperture indicated. For example, if the guide number for a flash unit is 160 with 100 ASA film and it is 10 feet from the subject then an aperture of f.16 is required, if the film in use is only 50 ASA then the aperture must be opened up one stop to f.11.

A basic studio set-up
Whichever system you decide on it is better to have at least two and preferably three light sources mounted on adjustable stands. One should be on a boom. This lets you position a lamp above the subject without the stand encroaching on the picture area. There is usually a choice of reflectors available. This ranges from a very soft reflector like an umbrella which gives a very

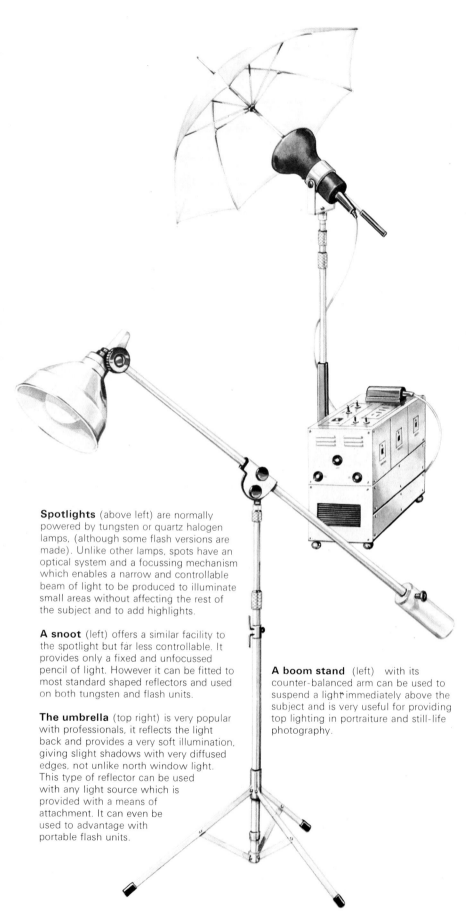

diffused light with soft-edged shadows, to a spotlight containing an optical system which can reduce the light to a narrow beam, producing dense shadows with hard edges. A convenient set-up which would enable a range of lighting effects to be achieved, would need one lamp with a standard reflector, one with a very soft reflector and a third lamp either with a spotlight attachment or a snoot, a cone which fits over the reflector so that the light can be directed into a confined or awkward area.

Even if only basic reflectors are available, it is a simple matter to vary the quality of their light with the use of a few home-made accessories. A diffusing screen is very useful. This is simply a frame over which is stretched translucent white fabric or tracing paper. When this screen is used between the light source and the subject the effect will be to produce a softer light. The effect can be varied by adjusting the distance between the light source and the screen, the further they are apart, the softer the light. A large diffusing screen of this type is an excellent way of simulating the effect of soft daylight and is a particularly effective means of lighting nudes, or indeed any subject where a natural lighting quality is usually desired.

An equally effective and even more simple accessory is a large reflector which can be a sheet of hardboard painted white—or even rigid card. Professional studios often use large sheets of white polystyrene three or four cm thick. These are quite rigid but very light and can be easily just propped against a chair or a lamp stand. One side of these can be painted black which can help to reduce the light reflected into shadow areas, where a more dramatic effect is required. These reflectors can be used close-up to the subject to reflect back the light from the main lamp, or another lamp can be 'bounced' off them for a stronger result.

The effect of a spotlight can be simulated by simply wrapping a cone of black card around the front of the lamp, although care should be taken that this does not become too hot. It is quite commonplace to see professional photographers with huge studios and masses of lighting equipment available, huddled into one corner playing around with the effects made by just a couple of lamps and reflectors.

Spotlights (above left) are normally powered by tungsten or quartz halogen lamps, (although some flash versions are made). Unlike other lamps, spots have an optical system and a focussing mechanism which enables a narrow and controllable beam of light to be produced to illuminate small areas without affecting the rest of the subject and to add highlights.

A snoot (left) offers a similar facility to the spotlight but far less controllable. It provides only a fixed and unfocussed pencil of light. However it can be fitted to most standard shaped reflectors and used on both tungsten and flash units.

The umbrella (top right) is very popular with professionals, it reflects the light back and provides a very soft illumination, giving slight shadows with very diffused edges, not unlike north window light. This type of reflector can be used with any light source which is provided with a means of attachment. It can even be used to advantage with portable flash units.

A boom stand (left) with its counter-balanced arm can be used to suspend a light immediately above the subject and is very useful for providing top lighting in portraiture and still-life photography.

Low light photography

The two main problems encountered with this type of photography is firstly the physical problem of reducing the risk of camera or subject movement, which is likely to result from the necessarily slow shutter speeds. By holding the camera correctly, making use of any additional support such as a wall, and releasing the shutter smoothly it is possible to make successful hand held exposures at 1/15 second or less. In really dim lighting you will need to use either much longer exposures and a firm tripod or to up-rate the film. Most fast films, both colour and black and white can be up-rated to two or four times their indicated speeds during processing, and most laboratories will provide this service if asked. Of course the image quality will be reduced, there will be an increase in grain and a corresponding decrease in definition, there is usually a reduction in maximum density with colour film which means weaker blacks and inevitably a loss of detail and gradation in shadows. However, the ability to shoot hand held pictures in almost any light that is good enough to read by, makes these disadvantages well worth putting up with.

The second problem encountered in low light level shooting is that of exposure assessment. This is caused by two factors, the first is that more often than not, light sources are included in the picture area, windows in interiors, and street lights for example, and if not allowed for, these can easily cause the exposure to be misjudged. The second factor is that this type of image is inevitably of high contrast, with bright highlights from light sources and often large areas of dark shadows. This invariably means compromise, since an exposure which is brief enough to record detail in the highlights will not be adequate to record shadow tones. The solution (apart from using additional lighting) is to choose a camera viewpoint and to frame the picture in such a way that such extremes are minimized. Light sources can either be excluded or sometimes hidden behind objects in the picture and large areas of dark shadow either avoided or utilized as part of the composition. Exposures must be calculated either from readings taken close-up from the most important area of the subject or by averaging readings taken from the brightest and darkest areas.

Reciprocity failure is something which becomes a problem when exposures increase beyond about 1/2 second. It simply means that the film no longer responds to the formula of twice the exposure equalling one stop lighter. If you calculate that an exposure of five seconds, is required it may be that in fact eight or ten seconds will be required.

For normal film exposures of one to five seconds a 50 percent increase should be tried, from five to ten seconds a 100 percent increase, and so on. This picture of a candle lit tomb, with some weak daylight, was given an exposure of ten seconds on daylight Kodachrome 25 on a meter reading of six seconds.

Pushed processing was used in this picture of a Parisian café scene to enable a hand held exposure of 1/15 seconds to be made. The film used was Kodak 400 ASA Ektachrome and the laboratory was asked to increase development to 800 ASA, a one stop increase. This service is available to most professional laboratories for a small extra charge.

Stage lighting presents an additional problem. As well as being of relatively low brightness, it is also highly concentrated, creating bright pools of light with dark areas between, making exposure assessment somewhat difficult. This picture of Max Boyce in concert was taken from the wings, which resulted in a certain amount of backlighting reducing the contrast slightly.

Illuminated buildings can produce quite striking pictures as this shot of the Arc de Triomphe demonstrates. The difficulty is sometimes that the exposure required for a brightly illuminated building is too little to record detail in the surrounding areas. One solution is to shoot while there is still some light in the sky. Another method is to choose a viewpoint and to frame the picture in a way that eliminates large areas of shadow.

127

Using studio lighting

It is a mistake to use more light sources than is necessary to achieve a particular effect. Nothing looks worse than a number of shadows each created independently by lights from different angles, criss crossing the subject.

Always start with only one light source, adjusting its quality and direction to reveal the qualities in the subject which are considered to be the most important. Once this lamp has been positioned to its greatest effect, further lamps or reflectors should be added only where and when they are needed, either to reduce the density of shadow areas, or to add additional highlights or modelling in the subject. But in any case they should be secondary to the main or key light.

One of the great advantages of shooting with studio lighting is that it offers total control over the result. Even with just a couple of basic lights and reflectors, it is possible to create a range of effects from shadowless high key lighting, to dramatic backlighting with dense shadows and strong highlights experiment for yourself.

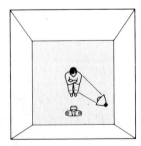

A standard 'studio' portrait, with interesting shadows, lit by the main light coming from one side (usually onto the model's 'best side').

A more subtle light achieved by positioning the light in the same place but diffusing it with a translucent screen. A sheet of tracing paper will do.

To separate the head from the background, use the screens and light but backlight with a spotlight.

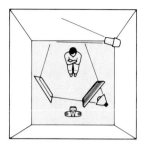

For a toned or high key use the light and diffuser screen as before but bounce the diffused light back towards the model. Use a white reflector screen of polystyrene or stiff, white paper.

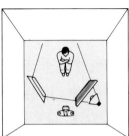

If you want more highlights use the screens and light as before but direct the spot to illuminate the model's hair.

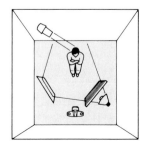

129

ARTIFICIAL LIGHT

A strongly directional light from almost at a right angle to the camera was used for this picture of a pensive man. It was slightly diffused by a tracing paper screen just in front of the lamp. To keep the shadow areas of the face very dense, a black reflector was used close to the model on the right. Even in a large studio, there will be a fair amount of stray light bouncing around and where solid black shadows are required, you must screen off this unwanted light.

A diffused light from the left and close to the camera was used in this portrait of a dark haired girl. A white reflector was also used, placed very close on the right of the model to keep the light on the face very open with a minimal amount of shadow. Then a second lamp was directed at her hair from behind and to the right to create a little sparkle. This was confined to the hair by taping a cone of black card to the lamp reflector so that only a small pencil beam of light was produced.

The slightly sinister effect of this shot of two young groovers was created by bouncing a single light from a white reflector on the floor just in front of the models feet. We are accustomed to seeing human faces lit from above eye level and when the lighting comes from a lower position it creates an unfamiliar modelling effect on the face. This kind of lighting is a rather more subtle form of the torch-under-the-chin technique children use at Hallowe'en.

The high key effect of this picture was created by directing two lamps, one from each side, at the white background. The models were lit by two reflectors placed either side of the camera. They were posed on a 'sweep' of white background paper which is simply a roll of wide cartridge paper hung from the wall and draped so that it curves on to the floor eliminating any join or angle which could create an unwanted shadow. To retain the high key quality, clothes were dispensed with and the only really dark tone in the picture is the girl's hair.

Lighting metal and glass

Some subjects require special consideration when lighting them. Glass for example both reflects and transmits light and when lighting glass it is usually necessary for both of these qualities to be shown. The usual method of lighting glass objects is first to arrange them against a white background some distance behind, and then to direct the main light source at this background. This will show the glass as transparent even tones, except at the edges or where there are mouldings or engravings. This alone can look extremely effective but to reproduce the true quality of glass it is also necessary to show its reflective nature. This can be done by bouncing an additional lamp, or lamps, off white reflectors placed close to the front of the still-life to create translucent highlights on the surface of the glass. Where the glass is lacking in detail, add darker tones to the

edges of the shapes by introducing dark reflector cards just outside the picture area but close enough to be reflected in the objects.

Subjects with highly reflective surfaces such as silverware can also present something of a lighting problem, especially when the surfaces are curved. The basic principle is to light them primarily by bouncing the lamps from large white reflectors, but where there are curved surfaces the shape of these reflectors will be seen on the surface of the subject. The solution to this is to totally enclose the arrangement inside a 'tent' of translucent white fabric such as tracing paper, with only a small hole through which the camera lens is aimed. The lights are then directed at the tent to create a soft overall tone without sudden changes in density, which in turn will be reflected in the surface of the objects.

The cutlery was lit by bouncing light off a large white reflector. The angle of the reflector, the cutlery and the camera was arranged so that the surfaces of the knife and fork literally reflected the illuminated reflector directly into the camera lens.

The most dramatic picture of the crystal (top left) was produced by bouncing a single light off the white background with no fill-in or additional lighting. The other shot was the result of simply adding a second diffused light source from close to the camera position and although it has less impact it gives a more accurate rendering of the quality of the glass.

The sweet dish was placed on a sheet of translucent perspex. A light source was directed from beneath it towards the camera. This is a useful technique for shooting transparent objects when a high viewpoint is required.

Using portable flash

The small, portable flash gun which can be tucked into the corner of a photographer's case has become one of the most widely used accessories. They are simplicity itself to use, particularly computer versions. They can however, be used in a way that can improve the results traditionally associated with small single flash guns on the camera, which are red-eyed, chalky white faces against pitch black backgrounds.

When using a direct flash with the gun mounted on the camera firstly insure that the subject is not too far away from background details. The illumination falls off quite considerably at greater distances from the flash and an exposure which will be correct at say two metres will be two stops underexposed at four metres. The second consideration is to avoid overexposure especially where skin tones are important, as it is very easy to lose detail and get that bleached out look with direct flash. It is particularly vital with flash on camera to ensure that the room or atmosphere is reasonably smoke free. This is difficult at a party or reception, but a smoke laden atmosphere will reflect the light from the flash resulting in a flat image similar to that of fog.

Another problem encountered with direct flash is the red-eye effect. This is caused by light being reflected back at the camera from the retina. It can be overcome by keeping the flash gun at a fair distance from the optical axis, if necessary holding or suppolting it slightly above the camera. This has the additional advantage of introducing a little more modelling into the subject.

A method of using a small single flash gun which is usually preferable to direct flash, is to 'bounce' it off a ceiling or wall onto the subject. Obviously when shooting colour it is vital that the surface used should be white, or at least neutral, and in any case quite light in tone. Naturally an increase of exposure is required as the light is travelling further and is being diffused by the surface which reflects it. The increase will depend on the distance of the flash from the ceiling or wall and then to the subject. The size and general tone of the room will also be a factor to consider, but as a general guide in a lightish room of say five by four metres and a white ceiling at three metres the increase required should be between two and three stops to give the best result.

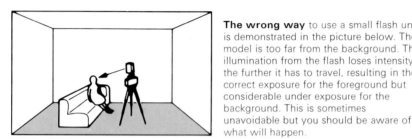

The wrong way to use a small flash unit is demonstrated in the picture below. The model is too far from the background. The illumination from the flash loses intensity the further it has to travel, resulting in the correct exposure for the foreground but considerable under exposure for the background. This is sometimes unavoidable but you should be aware of what will happen.

A better solution is to move the subject close to the background where possible. Subject and background will then receive almost the same amount of light and the correct exposure can be given for both. It also helps if, as in this case the flash is held slightly above the camera.

The best way of using a small portable flash is to bounce its light from a suitable surface such as a white ceiling. This has the advantage of giving a more even spread of light and a softer light which avoids dense hard-edged shadows.

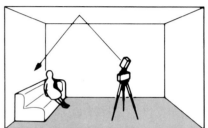

Flash and daylight

One of the advantages of electronic flash is that it can be mixed with daylight when using colour film, and even a small gun can be used effectively as a means of either controlling contrast or adding a little extra light in poor conditions. In both cases the principle is to calculate the exposure required for the natural light, and to use a shutter speed which allows the correct aperture to be used for the flash exposure. For example, if the exposure required for the daylight was 1/125 second at f.11 but the exposure for the flash required an aperture setting of f.5.6, then an exposure of 1/500 second at f.5.6 would fulfil both requirements.

If the camera shutter will not synchronize with the flash at this setting, then the flash must be moved closer to the subject thus allowing a smaller aperture and slower shutter speed to be used.

It is in fact unlikely that both exposures would need to be perfectly balanced in this way. A more natural result is given when the flash exposure is slightly less than the 'correct' one, this is particularly true when the flash is being used to even up excessive contrast in the lighting, as in a backlit portrait.

When the exposure ratio is reversed and the daylight exposure is reduced and the full flash exposure is given, the result tends to look artificial, but there are situations where it can be used effectively. If you wished to photograph someone with a sunset in the background for example, the exposure that would give adequate detail in the face would result in an overexposed and washed out sunset. In these circumstances the best effect would be achieved by reducing the daylight exposure to record detail in the sunset (underexposing) and using the correct flash exposure to illuminate the face.

An underexposed picture taken in daylight in conjunction with a flash unit on the camera has resulted in a deliberately artifical effect (top left). The overall exposure was given to produce an image two stops underexposed and the aperture was selected to produce a small degree of overexposure with the flash. The fall off in light from the flash has been increased by the fact that a wide angle lens was used and the flash has illuminated only the central part of the image.

Backlighting has produced an image with inadequate shadow detail in the picture of the dog (right), more exposure would have resulted in more detail in the shadows but would also have totally bleached out the background and the outline of the animal. The solution (far right) was to give the same overall exposure, but to also add light to the foreground by using a small portable flash unit on the camera. A shutter speed was selected which enabled the correct aperture to be used for the flash exposure. This was calculated to be slightly less than 'correct' exposure, as to give too much flash exposure would result in an artificial effect.

Camera shake has been deliberately used in the picture of a tree. The shot was taken at dusk. A shutter speed of about 1/25 second was chosen, which enabled the correct aperture to be used for the flash exposure. When the picture was suitably framed, it was vibrated by just trembling the hands and the shutter release during this process. The flash, which has a very brief duration, has frozen part of the image recording it quite sharply. The elliptical bright line in the top right corner is in fact the moon.

BASIC CINE

Making films is truly the synthesis of technology and creativity. To many of us, the process of creating a film has always seemed remote, difficult, complex and expensive. However, the introduction of the Super 8 film format 12 years ago helped to revolutionize amateur and home filmmaking. Based on a simple, pop-in cartridge and a 50 percent increase in available image size, the Super 8 format quickly found world-wide acceptance with home moviemakers.

This acceptance was greatly encouraged by the technological innovations built into the new cameras made to take Super 8. These included automatic light metering and exposure control, very fast, and long, motor-powered zoom lenses, slow and accelerated motion filming, time lapse photography, animation, macro-cinematography, special effects such as fades, dissolves and super-impositions and single system sound recording right on the film alongside the picture. Suddenly the creative tools of the professional filmmaker were available 'at the touch of a button' to anybody, at the price of a good still camera.

Of course, this is correct up to a point. By pushing a few buttons, anyone can create moving images and sound on film. However, without planning and without at least some familiarity with the technique, mechanics and language of film, these images will never become coherent presentations. Film after all, is one of the most powerful methods of communication. With some basic understanding, the filmmaker can not only represent 'reality', but can also modify any given reality to fit his vision of the world.

The Filmmaking Process

Even the most simple silent film usually follows a three stage evolutionary process: scripting, production and post production.

Scripting is the process whereby an idea or concept is translated into a road map for the finished film. Depending on the complexity of the film and the sophistication of the maker, this may result in a one page outline of 'forget-me-nots' or a thorough shooting script with specific instructions, dialogue, etc.

During the production phase, the script is translated into film. The film is shot. This again could be a simple, one-person operation or a coordinated effort of cameraperson, soundperson and director. When

this stage is completed, the film will be 'in the can.' All sequences will have been shot (often in several alternate 'takes') and sound will have been recorded.

Post production is really the editing phase. Using the script, the editor constructs the film from its picture and sound elements. It is an extremely creative process, demanding a great deal of skilful manipulation of the timing and continuity of scenes and the intelligent ordering of the organic structure of the film so that, when finished, it more or less represents the original concept.

Unlike still photography, the incredible number of variables in the making of even a simple film requires many compromises. Any

filmmaker soon learns the basic truth of filmmaking: you start out to make the best film ever made; during the shooting you compromise and hope for at least a good film; by the time the film is being edited, you are happy to have any sort of film at all.

Basic Equipment

You can make films with very little equipment. The basic requirement is a camera, a projector, a film viewer, and a film splicer. Most new cameras sold today can be used to make films with or without sound. A sound projector can, of course, also run silent film. Generally speaking, silent filmmaking is less expensive than sound filmmaking equipment although the price difference is not very great. If you are buying new equipment, think about getting a sound camera and projector. Sound need not add great difficulty to the filmmaking process but it does extend the enjoyment of the medium tremendously. As you can make silent films on sound film equipment, but not generally the other way round, the following equipment and techniques are discussed in terms of sound filmmaking.

What running speed should I use?

Most movie cameras, except the very cheap models offer a variety of filming speeds. For single system sound work, 18 and 24 fps are the only speeds to use. In fact, sound cameras will not record sound at any other speed. Most will not even run a sound film cartridge except on 18 or 24 fps.

Unless you plan to enlarge your Super 8 film to 16mm, transfer it to videotape or intend it for rearscreen projection in Fairchild, MPO Videotronic or technicolor machines, all of which require 24 fps, 18 fps sound speed is perfectly acceptable. What's more, instead of two minutes 30 seconds running time per cartridge at 24 fps, you get three minutes 20 seconds at 18 fps, although 24 fps will produce higher fidelity. Shooting 18 fps, will also reduce the amount of light needed to shoot: commonly, 18 fps may have an equivalent exposure of 1/28 second and 24 fps has 1/50 second.

Given a choice, slow motion speed is probably more desirable than speeds less than normal. Slight slow motion, such as 36 fps, will take the edge off potentially jerky movements (aerial or car filming) or provide just enough extra screen action (sports events) without making it unreal. True slow motion, which is a must in filming sport with multiple

cameras, needs 70 fps to really stretch the time of fast actions; 54 fps is not slow enough.

Speeds below 18 fps, excluding timelapse speeds of 2 fps and below, are not terribly useful except in low light static situations. Under such circumstances, the lower shutter speed may permit filming where it would otherwise be too dark. Filming movement at these speeds will serve to accelerate the action and compress real time into shorter screen intervals. This may be useful in traffic studies, for example, but is most often used in excess to provide comic effects.

The very slow speeds below 2 fps really begin to compress time (2 fps by a factor of 12 and 1 fpm by 1,440). Studies of slow moving phenomena like weather clouds become possible. In addition, the very slow speed can show action that, when normally viewed, shows no particular pattern or movement.

Finally, single frame capability is mandatory for animation. Using a cable release, you can expose the film one frame at a time, at will, while you animate your subject.

138

The camera

Even the least expensive movie cameras are loaded with buttons, knobs, scales and meters. The novice, on seeing a movie camera, gulps and thinks 'I'll never be able to make a decent movie. I'll never be able to make any kind of movie. Although it's true that many modern movie cameras look technically intimidating, all of them have been designed to permit simplicity of operation comparable to the average 35mm still camera. That is not to say that filmmaking has to be simple, only the operation of the camera has been simplified. In practical terms, this means that the filmmaker can concentrate on his subject and need not worry too much about the camera. Nevertheless, a basic understanding of the optical and sound system as well as of some special features will help you to translate what is in your head to what will appear on the screen.

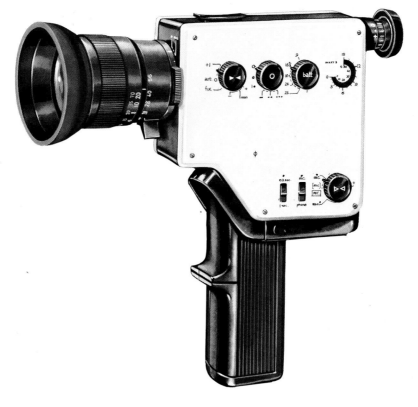

The Nizo 2056, a sound camera that can be used for single or double system sound filming.

The Fuji 2C1000 moviemaking system in its entirety. This is a single 8 system. Single 8 has a different cartridge design and uses polyester film stock, but when developed it is identical with Super 8. All the accessories for this system are available for Super 8 systems

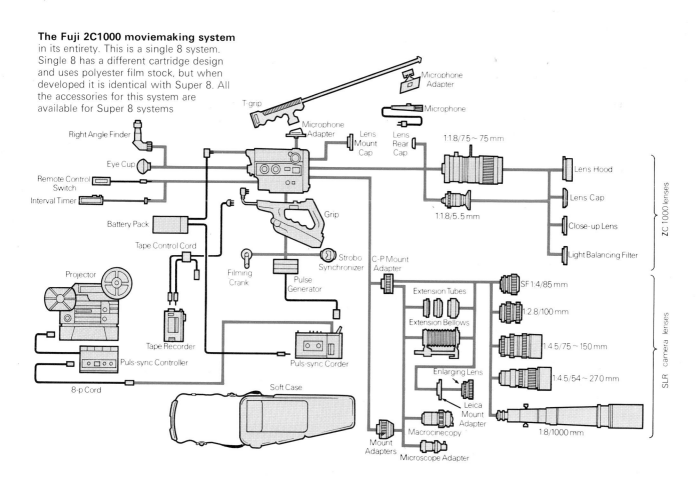

The optical system

The optical system consists of the zoom lens, the metering system and the viewing system.

Zoom lens

All Super 8 cameras have zoom lenses of some kind. A zoom lens is a variable focal length lens permitting the focal length to be set at any setting between maximum wide angle and maximum telephoto. The lens may be zoomed manually or electrically. A zoom lens is usually described by the ratio between maximum wide angle and maximum telephoto. For example, a 7 mm to 56 mm zoom lens has a ratio of 1:8 (equivalent in 35 mm still photography to a 35 to 280 mm lens).

Most zoom lenses have a minimum focussing distance of about 1.75 metres and may permit focussing as close as the surface of the lens when switched to the macro mode. All zoom lenses retain focus of a subject throughout the entire zoom range if the subject is initially focussed on maximum telephoto. This point is crucial to remember: **focus a zoom lens only at the maximum telephoto position.** Countless films have been ruined because the filmmaker focussed on the wide angle settings and then zoomed to telephoto.

Most zoom lenses have adequate sharpness throughout the zoom range and at all apertures. However, sharpness of most lenses decreases noticeably at maximum wide angle settings, at maximum apertures and at very small apertures. Usually zoom lenses are at their sharpest of f.4 to f.5.6.

Just as with still cameras, cine lenses have diaphragms for the control of exposure and depth of field. Most cameras have aperture ranges from about f.1.4 to f.22. Some XL cameras may even have a maximum aperture of f.1.1. The aperture is usually automatically controlled, but most cameras permit manual override.

Viewing system

The viewing (and exposure) system on virtually all Super 8 cameras is TTL. What you see is what you get. Focussing is straightforward, employing the conventional microprism and split image systems. Most filmmakers will not have any difficulties with focussing cameras, but

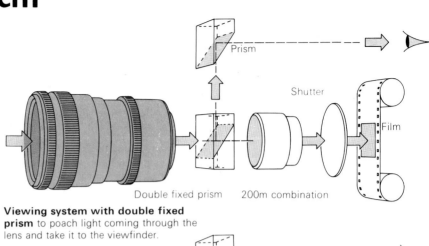

Viewing system with double fixed prism to poach light coming through the lens and take it to the viewfinder.

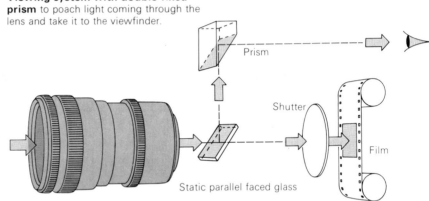

Viewing system with parallel mirrors to pick up light for the viewfinder.

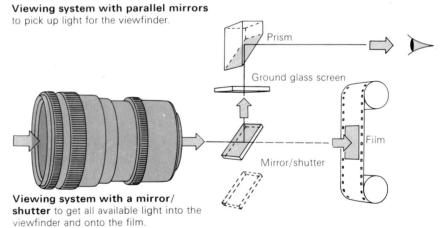

Viewing system with a mirror/ shutter to get all available light into the viewfinder and onto the film.

What is XL?

XL is currently the magic word in camera design. It implies that you no longer need to worry about the amount or quality of light on your subject. Wrong! XL or 'Existing Light' cameras simply optimize certain design factors so that a visible image may be produced at low light levels This 'optimizing' also degrades the image, because filming occurs at the outer limits of lens and filmstock design. That is not to say that XL is terrible, it is a very useful feature. Just remember, though, you never get something for nothing.

The XL designation usually combines the following elements: very fast lenses, usually f.1.1 or f.1.2; an increased shutter angle from 165° to 230°; running speeds of 18 rather than 24 fps; high speed 160 ASA film.

All this techno hardware will enable you to shoot with two to four f stops less light than normal.

too many forget about a little item in the viewing system called the diopter. Apart from not focussing on 'telephoto' with a zoom lens, not properly setting the diopter accounts for most of out-of-focus shots.

A diopter is a corrective optic within the viewing system that functions exactly like, and may replace, eyeglasses. You can set the diopter to duplicate the correction you get from your eyeglasses (if you wear them) and then be able to focus and shoot *without* your eyeglasses on. Or, you can wear your eyeglasses when you set the diopter and then shoot *with* your eyeglasses on. The choice is up to you but in either case, if the diopter is not set properly, the scene in the viewfinder will look very sharp after you have focussed but the film will be out of focus. Even if you do not wear eyeglasses you must adjust the diopter for your eyes. If someone else uses the camera, they must set the diopter for their vision. Don't forget to reset it for your eye when you get the camera back. Follow the instructions closely to set the diopter.

Metering system
The automatic metering systems of most cameras are excellent and should be used. However, there are common pitfalls.

Supposing you are filming a person talking in close-up and then you zoom out to show him standing against a white wall or against the sky. The second the light meter senses the sky or light wall, it adjusts its exposure for this brightness. The result is a nice blue sky, but a completely underexposed person. If you are planning a scene and there are changes from shadow to light areas, the meter will attempt to compensate and 'undulate' exposing neither shadows or highlights properly.

Anytime that you film a scene in which the light level of subject and background are dramatically different, the automatic metering will react to the bright area and underexpose the dark area. For situations such as these, use manual exposure and remember that on telephoto your zoom lens acts as a spot exposure meter.

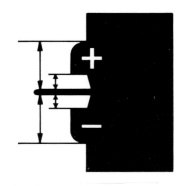

An automatic metering system for measuring the correct aperture.

Autofocussing movie cameras
Almost every manufacturer now builds at least one model movie camera with an auto focussing device. Most are based on the Honeywell Visitronic autofocussing module which uses rotating mirrors that react to changing contrasts for focussing information. The system works quite well, although, as with auto exposure and auto recording level control, it too can help produce unwatchable films. It does not react quickly to movement or dim filming conditions. Autofocussing has a tendency to 'hunt'. Nevertheless, it does exist and it is fun to use.

200 ft cameras
The most exciting development in movie cameras is the appearance on the market of more and more cameras capable of taking the 200 ft silent or sound Kodak cartridge. Not everyone needs the extended running time of course, but if you are a documentary filmmaker, 200 ft capacity can be a real boon. At 18 fps, a 200 ft cartridge will run for 13.5 minutes (10 minutes at 24 fps). However, it does require more power than the 50 ft cartridge, and the external battery pack option is definitely recommended.

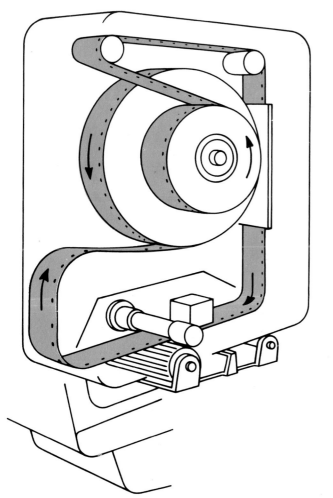

Film

Magnetic stripe

Capstan

Pressure guide

Anatomy of a Super 8 sound cartridge
This one is made by Kodak. It is available in 50 ft (15.2 m) or 200 ft (61 m) sizes and for tungsten or daylight light source. (Courtesy Eastman Kodak.)

Lighting

The essence of the film image (moving or still) is light. It is the correct and creative control of the light (available or artificial light) coupled with a basic understanding of exposure that is one of the key skills in the craft of filmmaking. This manipulation of light is often the filmmaker's signature on a film.

The introduction of XL cameras and high speed film emulsions has not changed this fact. True, when using a camera equipped with an f.1.2 lens and shooting on high speed Ektachrome 160 Type G film, the amount of light needed for exposure is reduced and colour balance becomes less critical, but the filmmaker must still decide how the available light is to be applied and optimized. The important factor is not whether the image is recognizable on the film but whether the image is of sufficient quality to convey the filmmaker's vision to the viewing audience.

No matter what the shooting situation, there is always something that the filmmaker can do to improve the image and give it life, solidity and visibility. At times, this may be as simple as changing camera angles or camera positions and metering the light manually. At other times, the judicious use of a bounced movielight or deployment diffused photoflood lamps can make a significant difference in the quality of the film. Add to that some inexpensive reflectors that help to direct the available light onto the subject or the background, and the image really begins to take on some tangible life.

Outdoors, under overcast or sunny skies, the filmmaker can also exercise considerable control over the available light. As beautiful as natural light may be, there are times when the application of filters, reflectors, diffusers or even some supplementary filtered light from a movielight help to control contrast, colour saturation and image definition in the film.

Movielights

Movielights are small, camera-mounted lights which usually contain a 650 watt quartz-bromine lamp. In use, the lights screw directly to the top of the camera and are usually designed to push the 85 filter out of the film path. Movielights are all made with tiltable heads that permit the light to be bounced. The better models have focussing control that allow the filmmaker to change the light from a fairly tight spot to wider flood position.

The best that can be said about movielights is that they do produce a nice bright light sufficient to expose Kodachrome 40 correctly at f.1.8 at three metres. The quality of the light, however, is something else. The illumination is extremely harsh and many hot spots exist that produce uneven results. When movielights are used as the single light on top of a camera, the results include very sharply defined shadows, a very bright central area and rapid fall-off into deep shadows beyond. If you are using high speed film, the movielight can be combined with some diffusion material which evens it out and makes the scene less harsh. Alternatively, bounce the light off the ceiling.

Photofloods and reflector floods

Without a doubt, the cheapest way to light for film is to use photofloods and reflector floods. The lamps are designed to fit standard lamp sockets and are manufactured in both the 3,400°K and 3,200°K light bulb version, or with a reflector built into the lamp. Most of them only burn for a few hours at the designated colour temperature and then slowly begin to drift toward the reddish end of the spectrum.

The attraction of these lamps goes beyond their thriftiness. The best thing about them is the wide variety of reflectors, barndoors and diffusion screens available from most manufacturers. The reflectors range in size from 12 to 30 centimetres and have a beam spread ranging from 40° to 100°. The reflectors may be stand-mounted or they may be attached to various inexpensive clamps and mounted anywhere.

Quartz lights

Most portable and lightweight film lighting equipment has been designed around small and efficient tungsten-halogen quartz lamps. The quartz lamp is superior to standard tungsten lamps such as the photofloods (whose life is only about six hours). The quartz lamp still has a tungsten filament, but is enclosed in an envelope of quartz glass filled

The only portable movielights available today are the Chinon XL20 and XL100 Lightfillers. They are cordless and rechargeable in about three to five hours. These lights enliven XL filmmaking by increasing sharpness and depth of field, and boosting colour brilliance.

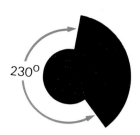

The shutter configuration on most XL cameras is 230° at the maximum. This does not mean you don't need lights when filming.

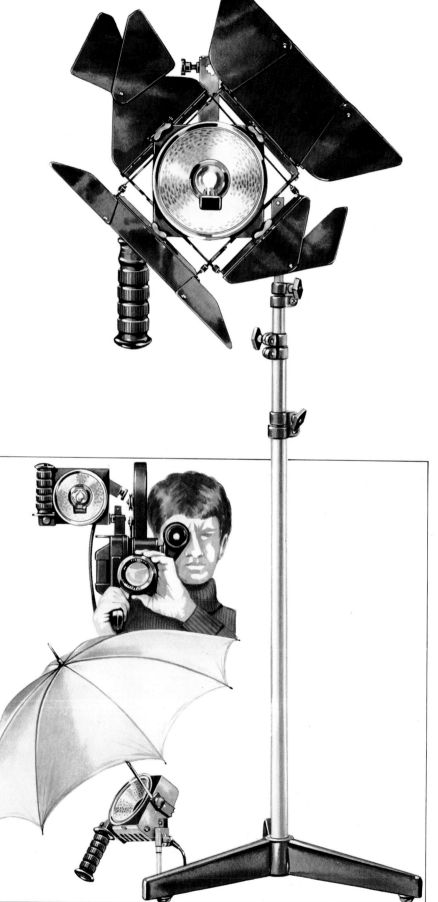

with a halogen—commonly iodine. The average quartz lamp burns for about 250 hours. Quartz lights cost more than other lights, but they offer the filmmaker the best control over the light on his subject. This does not mean that every home movie maker should rush out and spend £400 on lights. Instead, he should consider lighting in the whole context of his filmmaking needs. Many applications never require lighting, others always do. You buy the best camera you can afford, so don't neglect lighting. It's the filmmaker's paint brush.

The quartz omni light which is focussable and adaptable, and comes with a wardrobe of barndoors. You can mount it on a stand, on the camera, or on the floor, or hold it in your hand. If you don't want the barn doors, diffuse the light with an umbrella.

Sound

The sound system of the average Super 8 camera consists of a recording amplifier, recording head, capstan and pinch roller, sound monitor output jack, microphone input and recording level indicator. It is much the same as a cassette tape recorder. The sound quality achieved with most cameras is excellent.

The sound is recorded on a magnetic stripe that runs alongside the edge of the film. Because film movement is intermittent and sound recording requires stable continuous speed, the sound on film is actually recorded 18 frames ahead of the picture to which it belongs. During this 18 frame interval, the intermittent stop and go movement becomes smooth enough to permit the recording of high quality sound.

Most cameras offer the option of either automatic or manual sound level control. For most applications, setting the level automatically works perfectly well. Manual levelling can be handy when the sound levels vary drastically or when there is considerable background noise. Under conditions like this, manual sound levelling will eliminate the effect known as 'breathing' where the auto level control is constantly searching for the proper level. More important than manual or auto level control are microphone technique and sound monitoring. The neglect of both of these is what has given sound film such a bad name.

The first problem with miking is the microphone. The vast majority of camera manufacturers provide an omnidirectional microphone with their cameras. As the name implies, omni microphones pick up sound just as well from the back of the microphone as from the front. And what is usually behind the microphone? A noisy, running camera, of course. The auto levelling system immediately locks on to this sound and before you know it, the voice that you are really trying to record is all but inaudible. To compound the problem, the filmmaker probably does not have a headphone plugged into the camera to monitor the sound and will not find out until the film is processed that his sound is awful.

The elimination of both these sound problems is very easy. When you get the camera home, throw the standard microphone furnished with the camera into the dustbin. For very little money you can buy a unidirectional or cardioid microphone (most camera manufacturers even offer these as options). These microphones pick up virtually no sound from the rear. Then try to get the microphone in as close to the sound source as you can without bringing it into the camera frame. Finally, use an earphone or headphone to listen to the sound that you are recording. The flashing sound level light only tells you that *some* sound is being recorded on the film, not whether it is what you want.

Of course, most cameras have many other features related to the optical and sound system. As you begin to understand the camera and the filmmaking process as a whole, the additional features such as time lapse, single frame exposure, fades, dissolves and multiple running speeds begin to be important. As you learn to use these features you find that your films begin to look more polished and professional.

The projector

The sound projector in Super 8 filmmaking is a very active participant in the process of creating the finished film. It is not just used to look at the finished film, but plays a role in editing and sound mixing as well. As with the camera, projectors have both optical and sound systems.

The optical system consists of a zoom lens (usually) and a high intensity tungsten halogen cold light source. Most projectors have a brightness of 100 or 150 watts. A good lens and 150 watts of light permit you to show a correctly exposed film beautifully on a screen up to two metres wide. Remember, however, that it is not always so important to have a large screen image. Often, especially if the film is a bit shaky and/or underexposed, projection on a small screen is more advisable. Most projectors also provide a low/high lamp switch. Projecting on low will usually double the life of the projection lamp. As these are very expensive, it's worth conserving them.

The sound systems on even medium-priced projectors are very sophisticated and versatile. Apart from playing back recorded sound, the projector is also capable of recording sound from a record player or tape recorder. Again the level control is automatic or manual.

An excellent feature found on many projectors is sound-on-sound recording. With it you can record a musical background, for example, and then superimpose a second track of sound over it by variable

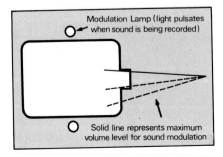

A single-system sound boom, made by Sennheiser. It is very light, very directional and fits most Super 8 cameras. Good clear sound is possible up to 10 metres away.

A sound level indicator located in the viewfinder of the Beaulieu 5008MS. The modulation lamp pulsates to indicate that sound is being recorded, while the solid line represents the maximum volume level for modulation.

Modulation Lamp (light pulsates when sound is being recorded)

Solid line represents maximum volume level for sound modulation

BASIC CINE

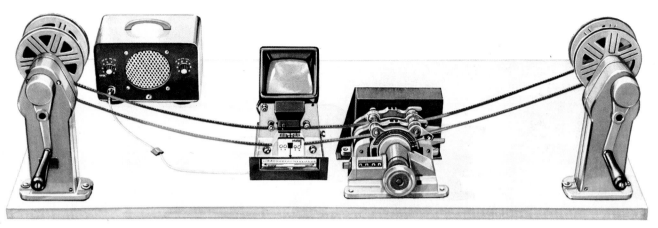

A double-system sound editing bench with a motorized synchronizer for holding the film in 'sync' during editing, a viewer, rewinds and an amplifier. A four strand version of this bench is available for more sophisticated editing.

A basic double-system sound filming set-up, showing a cable synchronized Nizo 2056 and a Super 8 Sound Recorder II. The camera can be used for single system.

The Norris 342 sound projector which is unique in having a series of foolproof control templates to lead the filmmaker through a prescribed mixing or sound technique.

erasure of the music. The process may be repeated several times to make a fairly complex multi-track.

All of this recording and variable erasing is fine if you start out with film that has no original sync sound recording on it. But what if you have a sound film with someone talking on camera and you wish to add music to the background? It is very difficult to do and the process usually destroys the original sound.

There is a solution, though. The new, dual track sound projectors. These projectors take advantage of the fact that sound film actually has two sound stripes—one on each side of the film. The balance stripe, originally put there to permit film to roll up evenly and to prevent scratches, can also record sound. With a dual track projector you never touch your original camera recorded sound and simply add the background music to the balance stripe. Some projectors even allow sound-on-sound recording on each sound stripe, as well as track-to-track transfers.

Editing equipment

Very few filmmakers create their films perfectly in sequence in the camera. Most films become films during the editing process. The primary editing tool is the film viewer.

The Viewer
Some viewers are motorized but most are manually wound. They all do the same thing: present the film to the filmmaker at any speed desired in such a way that poor sections can be removed, sequences rearranged and the film repeatedly viewed without subjecting it to the strains of a projector.

There are many viewers on the market and many are worse than junk. Take as much care in selecting your viewer as you do your camera. Cheap viewers not only give a poor picture but may also damage your film. It's always a good idea when buying a viewer to take along some film and thread it into the viewer. Look for these points:

Is the thread path simple?

When inserting the film in the viewer gate, do you have to drag it over the sprockets?

How is the frame marking accomplished? Via a punch on the edge of the film or by punching

a hole right through the frame?

Is the picture sharp and bright and are there focus and framing controls?

Is there a film pressure plate to hold the film flat?

Are there any rough edges that can scratch your film?

Does any part of the viewer make contact with the film other than the edges?

Can the viewer be adapted with an accessory sound head for sound editing?

Treat yourself to the best viewer you can afford. After all it is in this machine that your film will spend most of its time. By the same token, you will spend many hours looking at that little viewer screen while editing your film. If the picture is

A rearscreen Super 8 sound projector, made by Bolex, for viewing in daylight. These are becoming increasingly popular and most manufacturers have a version. Most of them can be instantly converted to front screen projection.

A Bolex V240M viewer, a standard type of viewer with manual winds. Accessories such as a sound head for single-system sound editing, are available for this model.

poor, so will your vision be after you finish your first film.

Splicers

The final component of a film-making system is the splicer. Once again, don't be a scrooge, buy a good splicer. What's the use of a good camera and long hours of shooting and editing if, when projected, every splice in your film becomes visible on the screen, or worse, breaks during projection. In addition to owning a good splicer, the filmmaker must also learn to make a good, clean splice. There are two splicing methods: cement (or wet) splicing and tape (or dry) splicing.

Cement splicing

Cement splices are best when sound filming or post-recording is done, if the original film will be extensively projected or when duplicates are to be made of the original film. Though a little more difficult to make than tape splices, cement splices are very definitely worth all the trouble.

You will need a high quality splicer in good adjustment and a lot of practice. A good splice will not come apart when pulled or twisted and is virtually invisible during projection from the original or from a print made from the cement-spliced original. The cement splice should also be thin enough to accept the application of a sound stripe without dropouts (momentary loss of the sound signal) at the join.

Almost any properly adjusted cement splicer will make a strong splice if the cement used is fresh, if the emulsion is thoroughly scraped to the film base and if the film is not pulled out of the splicer before it has dried properly. Even if you use a perfectly adjusted splicer, the splices may still show if too much cement has been applied. Strictly speaking, film cement does not glue the film together in the conventional sense. Film cement is a chemical solution containing solvents that partially dissolve, then fuse together the overlapped film ends. Excess cement evaporates. Good splices are usually as strong as the film itself.

The application of film cement is a crucial business. Just the right amount—not too much or too little—must go on. Too much and the cement will splash into the adjoining frames and make the splice visible on projection. Too little and the splice may come apart. Either problem will quickly become evident. After making a splice, let it set a while and then give it the usual twist and pull test to insure that it will hold. If the splice is going to break, it will usually fail this test, but that is better than breaking in the middle of projection.

Since the Super 8 splice is so small, it makes sense to apply the film cement with a very tiny brush. Most brushes that come with bottles of film cement are too large and will make messy splices. A nail polish brush and its bottle would suit better. Buy the cement in pint bottles and frequently dump the cement out of the small working bottle and then refill from the pint container. Film cement evaporates very rapidly during use and consequently quickly loses its effectiveness.

Tape splicing

For most filmmakers, tape is the most convenient splicing medium. It is quick and you never lose a film frame because all tape splicers are 'butt' splices and cut on the frame line. Tape splicers may use rolls of splicing tape or preperforated wrap-

ped individual splices. Given a choice, the prewrapped tapes are the best. Splicers designed for this tape usually pull the wrapper off, fold the splice around the film and even roller the film to make the splice tight. There is very little chance to do a sloppy job or to trap dirt under the splice. All splicers are designed to leave the sound stripe of the film uncovered. The new dual track splicers leave both the main and the balance stripe free of tape.

There are two main drawbacks to tape splicing. The first is the natural inclination of tape splices to pull apart slightly at the splice point. This also means that if the film has sound on it, there will be sound dropout at each pulled splice. This causes awful problems during post-recording of the film. The second problem with tape splices is with projectors. A good number of them have trouble maintaining proper projection loop and sound quality with tape splices. Check projector reputations on this point if you wish to tape splice your films.

Poorly made tape splices may pull at the splice joint, causing a white light to flash on the screen. Ragged or dirty splices will show up on projection and spoil the continuity.

The Hahnel type splicer which takes interchangeable tape cassettes to permit splicing of both single and double track film on the same machine.

Scriptwriting

Moved by a concept or a vision, a Super 8 filmmaker can grab a camera and start shooting. In later editing, the vision may be revised or expanded. The edited film may creatively evolve to present a view different from the one seen through the camera viewfinder. Reshooting or additional shooting may be necessary. A film may start with some planning but progress with a lot of inspiration and spontaneity. The editing is open-ended.

The Super 8 filmmaker is both camera operator and editor. As his experience in both worlds grows, his filmic sense grows with it. In the film industry, an editor is seldom behind a camera and a camera-person is seldom at an editing table. The Super 8 filmmaker has a chance to become a complete filmmaker. By cutting his own footage and then observing the flow and continuity of the film, he becomes more adept at cinematography, checking for smooth transitions as he starts and ends shots and anticipating footage that can be used to extend the time for a voiceover narration. He learns to keep direction of movement visually intelligible, to sense 'screen time' rather than real time when shooting, to create variations from the concept which may work out better in editing and, in general, to be able to mentally edit his film as he shoots it. This involves developing a grasp of the film as a whole and fitting each shot into its place in the overall scheme.

The process of scriptwriting is simply a more formalized version of determining what a good cinematographer and editor do naturally. Scriptwriting is not a must on each film, but is a process born of necessity. If the film concept is complex, if large numbers of people are involved or if the production time scheduling is stringent, a script may become necessary.

There are a number of ways in which films can find their way onto paper: a script treatment, a film script, a shooting script and a storyboard. Each is progressively more detailed and thought out, and each serves a different purpose. Needless to say, the nature of the production and the circumstances in which it is undertaken will determine either the necessity or the advisability of producing one of these script forms.

As a pure exercise in 'thinking film', working out a detailed script, 'testing' it on the shoot and comparing it with the final edit can be invaluable in acquiring the skills needed to execute a film which communicates the original concept on its own.

Film treatment

This is a narrative description of a film. It spells out the preliminary concept. It describes in brief terms both the objective of the film and its content. It then relates exactly how the filmmaker intends to accomplish his objective in terms of cinematography and editing. Often, the finished film may be quite different from the one described in a treatment, but the process of making the film evolves from this initial description of the film and its methods.

A film script

A scene-by-scene description of a film. It must include what will be said or heard and its relationship to what will be seen. It can take the form of a page with a line drawn down the middle. On the left is a description of the picture, or what will be seen. It also details the viewpoint of the camera and states when a shot is to zoom in or frame a person in a C.U. (close-up), M.C.U. (medium close-up), L.S. (long shot), etc. The picture described on the left will be seen at the same time that the dialogue or narration on the right is being heard. Transitions from scene to scene (dissolve to, cut to, fade out) are written out between each scene. This is ideal for any film which attempts to communicate a clear concept, such as a promotional, educational or training film.

Another way of writing this type of film script is simply to write it in narrative form, describing camera moves along with action and dialogue in story form. For example: 'Camera closely follows John's hand as he slowly picks up and grips the knife. Cut to Richard's face as his mouth curls in hatred. Richard advances, his face slowly filling the scene and going out of focus. Only Richard's steps are heard'. This type of script is best suited for dramatic films where the emphasis is on combining dialogue, acting and cinematography to establish a certain mood or effect.

Shooting script

This supplies the exact detail for each shot, transition and word spoken. It is the camera operator's

| John's hand slowly picks up the knife | Cut to Richard's face as his mouth curls with hatred | Richard advances towards camera |

A homemade storyboard to map the progress of a dramatic home movie.

'map' to the film. In order to write a shooting script, the limits of the location of the shoot must be taken into account. The cameraperson will know ahead of time whether there are windows in an interior, and if so, whether or not he plans to place someone near them. He will have decided ahead of time whether the drapes will be shut. The placement of both the camera and the subject will be worked out from shot to shot. If a voiceover narration is to coincide with someone demonstrating a process, the narrative will be exactly timed. When the process is acted out, the cameraperson has someone watching a stopwatch and coaches the actor to time his moves to match the narration. In working out such a detailed script, many problems become apparent that can be solved before the shoot begins. For instance, one piece of narration may take 45 seconds to speak, but the scene that is to play along with it does not contain enough action to be interesting for the full 45 seconds. The scripting stage, rather than the editing, is the proper point for deciding how to handle this situation. The writer may decide to cut the narration and state the information more succinctly, or he may call for several new scenes or cuts to keep the film flowing during the full narration.

When a shooting script is developed, as little as possible is left undecided. This allows the filmmaker to devote full attention to getting each shot just right and to work for the best performance or reading. Without a shooting script, much of the filmmaker's time and energy is spent in on-the-spot improvization. With each variation between the original script and what is actually shot, he changes another piece in the puzzle and risks having to make drastic revisions or omissions in the editing.

Storyboard
This goes one step further than a shooting script. Here each camera angle and scene is sketched out with the narration or dialogue written under it. Focal lengths, depth of field, exact timing, dress, props, coordination of words and movements are all spelled out. Television commercials are representative of projects requiring this treatment. Because they cannot be even a fraction of a second over or under their allotted time, the final edit must perfectly reproduce the original.

Cinematography

Cinematography is the means of translating the written word of the film script into the images and sounds that are later edited together to form the completed film. It encompasses camera operation, composition, camera movement, continuity and lighting. Mastery of a few simple basics will strengthen any film.

Camera operation
To make the camera work for you, you must overcome any fear, awkwardness or unfamiliarity with it. Some people never feel comfortable with a machine, but to be effective, you must make the camera an extension of yourself. You must explore every capability that it offers and not be afraid to try things that seem unconventional. During a shoot, you should be so at ease with the camera that most of your energy can go into concentrating on the action before you. You should never be so preoccupied with running the camera that you let the action take second place.

Focussing
When focussing, remember that virtually all Super 8 cameras have zoom lenses. All zoom lenses are designed to hold focus throughout their total zoom range, provided that the initial focussing of the subject has been done with the lens at its longest telephoto setting. If you are shooting without zooming on

some in-between focal length, focus first on telephoto then move back to your selected focal length.

Metering
Remember that cameras with TTL metering make very fine spot meters. By zooming in to full telephoto, critical areas of any scene can be quickly metered. Based on these spot readings, the filmmaker can then decide how to modify the initial average reading. In general, manual metering results in more accurate exposures than slavish automatic metering. This is especially important when the camera is moved during a take so that its field of view takes in areas of varying brightness. Automatic meters will respond to such brightness by undulating. As a dark or bright area comes into the field of view, the exposure system begins to correct in a slow and gradual manner. The effect will be unpleasant because the exposure change destroys the relative balance between the shadows and the bright areas.

Handholding
Because Super 8 cameras are light and small, handheld operation seems ideal. This is true if you take a few steadying measures. Stay away from those long telephoto shots. Any small movement will become magnified. If you have any choice, frame the shot to include as few horizontal or vertical lines as possible. These

Use a friend to stabilize for a long telephoto shot.

provide visual references to camera unsteadiness. Wide angle shots generally appear smoother than telephoto shots. When you hold the camera, hold it firmly but not tightly. Any body tension is translated into camera shake. The best position is to hold the camera with your elbows tucked under the camera for support. If there is a wall, tree or rock nearby, lean against it for extra steadiness. If you are filming in a moving car, do not lean against the back seat. Use your arms as shock absorbers and isolate the camera from the car's vibrations. Often, letting a little air out of the car's tyres before the shoot will result in a smoother ride.

Zooming

Although zooming the camera lens produces no real movement, many filmmakers think that it does. Every Super 8 camera has a zoom lens of some kind. In some, the function is motorized, others are manually operated. Undeniably, it is fun to zoom, but usually only for the cameraperson. For the most part, the zoom produces empty movement that does not further the artistic process of the film. The illusion of movement is created by increasing or decreasing the magnification of the subject. The image is very flat since camera-to-subject distance does not change and no objects actually move past one another (as in a dolly shot). With a zoom there is the feeling that the centre of interest is either pulled towards the viewer or pushed away. On the whole, the zoom does little to make a scene three dimensional.

Zooms are most effective when they are done very slowly, and when the zoom moves from the telephoto position to the wide angle position. In this way, the telephoto subject's relationship to his environment can be established while the viewer has time to examine it and make connections. Conversely, moving the other way, from a slow wide angle pan to a zoom into the area where the action is taking place can also work very well as an establishing shot. Here too the key is slow zooming. Some workers have used extremely fast zooms (zaps) as transitional devices where a fast zoom to a subject is followed by a cut.

The real strength of the zoom lens lies in its ability to make possible an infinite number of focal lengths without changing lenses. Framing, composing and establishing depth

A zoom sequence pulls the subject towards the audience.

of field are all made easier. By focussing at maximum aperture and telephoto, and then zooming back to the desired focal length, maximum sharpness is ensured. If the camera meters through the lens, the zoom feature helps to turn it virtually into a spot meter by allowing light readings at full telephoto. Lighting ratios, contrasts, etc. can be quickly established and the right exposures calculated. A good rule might be to zoom only between takes.

Panning and tilting

A pan shot is made when the camera is moved horizontally on its axis.

The tilt shot is made when the camera is moved vertically. Both the tilt and the pan shot are most effective when they are done smoothly and slowly or when they are swished rapidly. In between, the movements may be too fast to take in the details of the panned or tilted area. If there is any movement in the scene, the camera move will strobe. This strobing is due to the intermittent movement of the film and the continuous action of the scene. Strobing is less pronounced at higher frame rates due to the fact that every second of movement is broken into more images.

It is a good idea to film a few seconds before beginning a pan or a tilt and to film for a few seconds after completing the move. This will give the editor the option of cutting either on the move or on the static shot. Slow deliberate pans are good for orienting the viewer. The details of the entire scene are presented one after the other in a way that allows them to sink in. Swishpans, on the other hand, are transitional devices that virtually drag the viewer along. No detail is visible; just dynamic parallel bands of colour and black-and-white that provide viewers with a strong sensation that they are being transported.

You can do pans and tilts with the camera handheld or on a tripod. If you do use a tripod, choose one with a fluid dampened head. This is the smoothest, although many friction head tripods also work well. If the friction head is not smooth and the camera has a 36 fps running speed, improve smoothness by running at higher than normal speed.

Handholding the camera during a pan shot is difficult, but you can improve smoothness by using a shoulder pod. For best results, the lens should be at the widest possible angle. The camera operator should be comfortable enough to maintain a stable position until the end of the pan. His feet should face the final direction of the pan while his upper torso faces the starting direction. During the pan, he slowly unwinds and muscle tension is reduced. At the end of the pan, the operator is comfortable and the camera is steady. Handheld telephoto pans usually suffer from severe shakiness.

A variation of the pan shot is the shot that follows the action by either panning or tilting. As a man walks or runs down the street, the camera follows. If the man walks away from the camera, he will get smaller. If he

Stabilize the camera with a fluid head and tripod (top) for panning. A Jones brace (above) lets you shoot smoothly on the run.

moves toward the camera, he grows larger. A shot like this may be difficult to focus unless sufficient depth of field is present. If not, follow focus must be used. If the action is fairly rapid (as with a man running or a car moving) the pan should lead the action a little bit. This gives the viewer some assurance that the subject will not exit unexpectedly. Compositionally, it also looks better. When following action, it is always a good idea to shoot before the subject enters the scene and continue shooting until the subject makes an exit. This is essential to avoid jumpcuts and to provide the editor with some options.

Trucking shots and dolly shots

Trucks and dollys are the most visually exciting shots. As the camera moves, objects in different places seem to move past each other and a feeling of three dimensionality is introduced. The dolly shot usually moves towards or away from the action while a trucking shot usually parallels the action. Camera moves may be achieved by utilizing everything from specially-built tracks to the handlebars of a bicycle.

Of course there are many more ways to move the camera during a shot. An inventive mind will have no trouble creating new moves. In addition to the basic moves discussed above, the camera might also be moved by rotating, jiggling, throwing or waving. Various combinations of pan-tilt, dolly-tilt-pan, zoom-tilt, pan-zoom, zoom-pan-tilt, etc. could be executed. You could walk or run with the camera. You could film from a moving cable car or, if you are brave enough, from a galloping horse. You can let the camera wander in a long shot, medium shot, close-up or even in a diopter shot. The camera can be strapped to athletes, performers or even animals for interesting point-of-view shots. If you can't think of any way to move the camera, then you can always move the actors. Or, better yet, move both.

Composition

Many still photographers who turn to filmmaking try to apply the rules of still picture compositions to film. As long as the image is static, this works well. However, film is not naturally static, there is movement through space and time. The camera moves, the subject moves or both move at once. Compositional elements that seemed balanced in a static situation suddenly change with movement. Camera angles and points of view change. Within a scene, as the action progresses, alternations between close-up, medium shots and long shots change the dynamics of the composition. Most important, in film there should be no virtuoso compositions that bring attention to themselves. Composition exists to further the action and development of the film. Every shot filmed relates to the shot before or the shot after and to the film as a whole. As with other rules, those of composition are usually successfully broken—but it helps to know a few of them first.

In any film composition, the movement within the film image works to create depth, giving the feeling that in fact the flat film image is three dimensional. But depth is also emphasized by lighting certain areas with the frame, by the direction in which action flows and by providing certain foreground or background elements.

Lighting is a very powerful compositional element. Backgrounds against which the subjects play can be made darker or lighter than the subject. This separates the subject from his surroundings. Appropriate and dramatic side lighting and backlighting can also position the subject in space and again separate him from his backgrounds. Often if it is not possible to completely light a room, the placement of area lights at various points will give the illusion of depth.

The most exciting filmic compositions are those in which the subject movement is towards or away from the camera. By using a wide angle, this movement away or towards the camera is emphasized. The telephoto lens compresses the space and seems to stop movement.

With subject movement parallel to the camera, even a moderate telephoto lens seems to accelerate the movement and blur the background. This can be very effective with good subject/background colour separations. The use of a wide angle lens in the same situation would seem to make the movement past the camera much slower.

Another strong compositional tool is the positioning of subjects within the frame in relation to foreground and background. The foreground can have another person, or tree branches, moving traffic, etc. Proper arrangement can greatly increase the dramatic tension or explain relationships between the subjects and objects of the scene.

A most important tool of composition is camera angle. There are a number of standard angles:

Eye level shot: the point of view of normal vision.

High angle shot: when the camera looks down from an angle above eye level. A shot like this can distort perspective and if a person is the subject can make him look weak, vulnerable, defeated or diminutive.

Low angle shot: when the camera looks up from an angle lower than eye level. As you would expect, the low angle makes people look big, powerful and dominant. It too distorts perspective.

Point-of-view shots (POV): the POV shot can be from any camera angle, but it is from the viewpoint of the subject. For example, a close-up of the subject's eyes looking up would logically be followed by the scene he was looking at from his point of view. Recently a film, *Dog's Day*, was shot entirely from the point of view of a Dachshund. A Super 8 camera had been strapped to the animal.

Here are some common sense compositional guide-lines.

Watch out for cut off heads and limbs. This does not mean that the entire body has to be in the frame all the time. When you cut off body parts, do it at the chest or the waist. When cutting limbs, cut them between joints rather than at the joints.

Make sure all vital visual information is in the scene. If you are shooting a child sitting on the floor and looking down as he plays, let the audience see what he is playing with.

Watch out for the background. Telephone poles coming out of people's heads look just as real on film as they do in stills.

Keep the frame of the camera lined up with vertical and horizontal objects in the scene.

When someone is moving in the

The ball provides the continuity even though the background changes dramatically from shot to shot. Remember that the ball must enter and leave the screen in the same direction every time.

scene, compose to leave a little extra room in front of their movement. In other words, if someone is running across the scene from right to left, keep the person composed on the righthand side of the scene so the viewer has sense of where he is going.

Eliminate distracting elements. If part of someone else is sticking into the corner of your scene or there is a lot of unrelated movement in the background, you should move around and look for a better angle from which to compose the shot.

Continuity

Except for out of focus films, under or overexposure or shakiness, the novice filmmaker's biggest problem is continuity. Continuity in a film means that each shot is so organized and balanced that the film will flow smoothly. The viewer should not be consciously aware of the film's structural elements. He should be carried along by the film even though

the film was not shot in sequence or at the same time of day or even in the same year. The transition from cut to cut should flow.

The classic continuity exercise is the bouncing ball routine. Start a football rolling from a closet at home and let it roll to the neighbourhood pitch. On its way, it can cross streets, pass through buildings and cross in time through seasons or nights and days. Its the movement of the ball in each cut that maintains the familiar and helps us to accept as natural the changing background.

Continuity, however, is not insured just by movement. The filmmaker also works with continuity of time (not just forward but also through flashbacks, time compression and expansion), continuity of space (or action moving from one location to another), continuity of direction (the direction in which a person looks, objects and people, etc). Continuity is helped along by such devices as fades, superimpositions, dissolves, titles.

Editing

Editing Super 8 film (even single-system sound film) is far easier than most people think. No longer does the filmmaker have to worry about lighting, composing, moving people around, getting people to talk and all the other details that can complicate the shooting process. The filmmaker or editor now has the creative and fun task of taking all the footage shot and arranging it into the film he wants.

To edit, you will need a viewer (with sound head if you are cutting sound movies), a tape or cement splicer (tape is recommended until the editing is final), some double-sided tape, a few empty reels, some film leader, and most important, pencil and paper. It is also useful to keep your projector handy so that as you are editing you can periodically watch the work in progress.

In preparation for your editing, you should take some leader or unwanted film and practice making splices, threading and marking on the viewer, and running a piece of film through the projector to test the splices you made.

To help keep your film clean you might also buy a few cotton film editing gloves, some film cleaner with lubricant and some pieces of lint-free flannel. Wear at least one editing glove while editing and handle the film only with that hand. This will prevent fingerprints which are impossible to remove easily, even with film cleaner, from ruining your film. Later, after editing is complete, use the flannel wet with a few drops of cleaner to clean and lubricate the film prior to projection.

The editorial sequence is fairly standard. How long it takes is up to you.

Splice the small individual rolls of film together on a big reel. It helps if the splicing is done in a logical sequence.

Project the film as often as needed for you to know all of it intimately.

While projecting make a log of takes and indicate whether they are good or bad.

Tape the double-sided tape on a convenient wall and above the tape, mark sequential numbers at 12mm intervals.

Put your film in the viewer and, guided by your screening log, cut out the scenes that you wish to use in the finished film.

Stick this piece of film onto a number on the double-sided tape. Only one frame needs to stick to the tape. If the piece of film is too long, roll it on a reel and number it.

Begin a log of good takes. Using the number assigned to each piece of film, describe it in the log.

After removing the piece of film to be hung up, splice your 'out-takes' back together and continue the process of selection and logging.

When the selection and scene log is complete, get a glass of wine and begin your 'paper edit'. The 'paper edit' is another selection process. Here you decide what scene comes first. In front of the log number you now write a sequence number.

Go back to your viewer and in the sequence determined during the paper edit, splice together the rough cut of the film. Remember to wear your editing glove, to work cleanly, to make your splices carefully and to attach at least one and a half metres of leader to the front and back (head and tail) of your film.

The fun now begins, and it's called fine cutting. This is where your sense of timing, continuity, and so forth will come into play. You slowly work your way from cut to cut, trimming excess and re-arranging scenes. You most probably will discover in this process that the piece of film that seemed just right, doesn't fit. If you were able to do multiple takes in your shooting, search through your reel of out-takes for a better shot.

Periodically clean the film and project it to see how it flows.

Continue this process of refinement until you are happy, exhausted or sick and tired of the whole film.

At this point, if the film is silent, you may want to remake the splices with cement and send this film off to the laboratory for sound striping. When the sound-striped film comes back, add whatever sound you have chosen and complete the film.

If you are editing a single-system sound film, the editing procedure is very similar except that you must now also base your selection criteria on what is said—as well as what you see. Because you are dealing with sound, six-frame montage cutting is out. The sound will often control your cutting. Also because the sound is 18 frames in advance of the picture, a certain editing and shooting methodology apply:

Your film and viewer must have a sound head so that you can hear the sound. Motorized viewers are helpful for sound because they keep the sound on-speed better than hand winding.

When you shoot a sound movie, start the camera but do not have your sound, dialogue or narration begin for *one second* after the camera starts. In editing, you will lose the first second of sound so while shooting, avoid having any important sounds occur in the first second of a scene.

When you edit, make your cut at the head of a scene on the sound track where you want the sound to begin. At the tail of a scene, make your cut on the picture where you want the picture to end. Remember when cutting, it is: *sound-head, picture-tail.*

Finally arrange a 'premiere' and sit back to enjoy your handiwork.

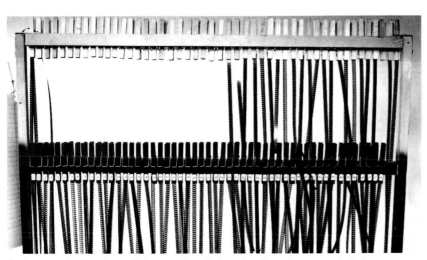

A cheap and effective editing rack made from brackets, battens and clothes pegs.

INDEX

Page numbers in italics
refer to illustrations.

INDEX

Acknowledgements

The publishers would like to thank the following individuals and organizations for their kind permission to reproduce the photographs in this book.

Photography by Michael Busselle.

Additional photographs by kind permission of:
Samson Low 82 below, Leo Mason 114–115, Gerry Cranham 116–117.

Basic movie photography and artwork reference by Gunther Hoos, 140, 141, 147, 149, 150, 151, 152, 153.

The following artists supplied illustrations:
Harry Clow, 12, 13, 14, 15, 16, 17, 19, 124, 125, 139, 141, 144, 145, 146; Phil Emms 13, 17, 24, 120, 121, 140, 145; Phil Holmes, 12, 13, 139; Dave Pugh, 142, 143; Technical Art Services 19, 128, 129, 134, 135; Colin Salmon 19, 100.

Equipment courtesy of:
Leeds Camera Centre

Cover Photograph:
Paul Williams